YORK NOTES

General Editors: Professor A.N. Jeffares (*University of Stirling*) & Professor Suheil Bushrui (*American University of Beirut*)

Keith Waterhouse

BILLY LIAR

Notes by Neil McEwan

MA B LITT (OXFORD), PH D (STIRLING)
Lecturer in English Literature, University of Qatar

LONGMAN
YORK PRESS

YORK PRESS
Immeuble Esseily, Place Riad Solh, Beirut.

LONGMAN GROUP UK LIMITED
Longman House, Burnt Mill,
Harlow, Essex CM20 2JE, England

First published 1990

ISBN 0-582-03822-7

Produced by Longman Group (FE) Ltd
Phototypeset by Gem Graphics, Trenance, Cornwall.
Printed in Hong Kong

Contents

Part 1

Introduction

The author's life

Keith Spencer Waterhouse was born at Hunslet, Leeds, in Yorkshire, on 6 February 1929, the youngest of five children. His father was a greengrocer. He attended Osmondthorpe Council School, Leeds, and left at the age of fifteen. In an introduction written for a later edition of his first novel, *There is a Happy Land* (Longman, 'Imprint Books', 1968), he tells us how, when he started to write fiction, his own childhood seemed unpromising material because 'I came from a world where nothing ever happened':

> My background seemed dull and unpromising . . . a dormitory housing estate of long, empty streets, a childhood that was neither desperately poor nor exotically wealthy . . . I looked up and down Middleton Park Grove, the quiet, featureless street where I was born. Where was the life? Where was the drama?

He found the life and drama in ordinary events and in the imagination which transformed them; *There is a Happy Land* and his second novel, *Billy Liar*, are indebted to memories of early life in Leeds. *Billy Liar* owes something to the years after leaving school when he had various unpromising jobs, including one as an undertaker's clerk. Then he became a reporter in Leeds and so started a long and distinguished career as a journalist.

He has been a prolific writer, not only in the field of the novel. He moved from Leeds to London in 1951 (after marrying in 1950), and has worked as a freelance journalist ever since, known to a very large readership as a columnist on the *Daily Mirror*, and the recipient of many awards (including the Granada Award, 1970, and the British Press Award, 1978). His first play for radio, *The Town That Wouldn't Vote*, was broadcast in 1951. The first of his books (written in collaboration with Guy Deghy), *The Café Royal: Ninety Years of Bohemia*, was published in 1955; *How to Avoid Matrimony* followed in 1957. The first of his many plays for television was *The Warmonger* (1970). There have been many since, including a series based on *Billy Liar* (1973–4). Some of these were in collaboration with the playwright Willis Hall (*b*.1929), with whom Waterhouse has also written more than sixteen plays for the stage. The first was an adaptation of

Billy Liar which was first performed in London (at the Cambridge Theatre) in 1960, and then in Los Angeles and New York in 1963. (A highly praised film, based on the novel, was released in 1963 and a musical adaptation, scripted by Waterhouse and Hall, was produced in 1974; adaptations of the novel are described in Part 4 of these Notes.)

Waterhouse's first novel, *There is a Happy Land* (1957), is written from the point of view of a boy of about ten. The boy, never named, is a gifted mimic who acts the parts of disabled and drunken adults and calls out mocking 'cheeky' comments, attacking the adult world with an irreverence that is characteristic of this novelist's heroes. *Billy Liar* was published in 1959; it is by far the best-known of Waterhouse's books. Billy is known even to people who cannot recall the author's name: this reflects the author's success in creating a character who has caught the popular imagination, and added, some would say, in an age when novelists have to struggle to find a readership, to the mythology of our time. Notable among later novels – *Jubb* (1963), *The Bucket Shop* (1968), *Maggie Muggins; or, Spring in Earl's Court* (1981) – is *Billy Liar on the Moon* (1975). All these books deal with fantasy and muddle in ordinary lives; all are satirically attentive to cliché and grammatical peculiarities in speech. Some are harsher in tone and more conscious of evil than *Billy Liar* and its sequel. In *Billy Liar on the Moon*, Billy is unhappily married, living in a council flat with his wife and mother (his father having died), working in local government in a small town, and, fifteen years after the day of his adventures in *Billy Liar*, still steeped in fantasy. The moon is a new townscape of shopping-arcades and housing estates. Like *Billy Liar*, the sequel is very funny.

General background

A novel describing details of social life and written thirty to forty years ago is likely to seem quaintly out of date, like the fashions and idioms of our parents' youth. The continuing popularity of *Billy Liar*, among young people as well as among readers for whom it has a nostalgic appeal, is a sign of strength. Yorkshire in the later 1950s sometimes sounds innocent, as in Chapter 10 where Saturday evening at a dance hall is conveyed by the image of 'squealing girls scoffing cream buns and spilling lemonade down their dresses'. Teenagers usually drink coffee. The 'passion pills' which Billy feeds surreptitiously to a girl are unlikely to be dangerous. Two youths are turned away from the dance hall, on the first page of Chapter 11, because Mr Bottomley has given strict orders to exclude them, following unspecified bad behaviour the week before. The commissionaire has no difficulty in enforcing this ban. In this small town, at least, violence does not seem to be a social problem.

There is a detail worth noticing in the commissionaire's appearance. He wears a threadbare uniform held together by an army webbing belt. Billy must have been born during the Second World War (Waterhouse was too young for the war, but did National Service in the R.A.F.); it is never out of his thoughts for long. He is divided between an impulse to mock, as in the army 'routine' which he and Arthur are given to enacting under the war memorial in Town Square (Chapter 3), and an opposite tendency to dream of himself as a war-hero. His fantasy-land of Ambrosia has recently been at war, and his thoughts on the first page of the novel mingle heroism with absurdity, as he pictures Ambrosia's victory march. The Billy of real life is a most unmilitary figure, but conspicuous among his lies is the story that his father was a distinguished naval captain and a prisoner of war. He belongs to a generation which grew up hearing and reading stories of 'the War', and commonly rejected in later adolescence attitudes and behaviour which could be labelled as 'militarism'. The only contemporary figure, outside the world of entertainment, whom Billy mentions with respect is Bertrand Russell (see Notes and glossary to Chapter 1, in Part 2 below). During the 1950s, a period of authority and patriotism was gradually yielding to one of a very different mood, to be labelled 'permissive' in the 1960s when all forms of authority became a popular target of satire. There were many reasons for the change, including the end of the Empire, the threat of nuclear war, and the loosening of the British class system. Billy is a modest and muddled rebel, but in some ways he is a representative figure of a time of transition.

Like his author, he is a Yorkshireman. Keith Waterhouse had left the city of Leeds to become a journalist and novelist in London; Billy wants to leave the small town of Stradhoughton, somewhere in Yorkshire, to write scripts for a London-based comedian. The society portrayed in the novel offers little to ambitious young people (except, it might be said, the opportunity to satirise it). Waterhouse's Yorkshire has exchanged one kind of poverty for another. Harsh conditions on low pay in woollen mills, coal-mines and factories, known in the industrial regions of the county from the eighteenth century until recent times and still remembered by the older characters in the novel, have become for Billy and his generation no more than a source of jokes. The new poverty is of two kinds. Cheap building, shoddy design and mass-produced materials are spoiling the town, its main streets coming to look like those anywhere in Britain, Billy fears. Even bleaker, the novel asserts, is the degeneration of English. The old dialect had some life and warmth in it. People today speak in clichés and are trapped within a 'blunt and blunted' way of speaking which denies all feeling and imagination. This is the dreariest feature of Northern life, more stupid and stultifying than any of Billy's lies.

Literary background

Kingsley Amis (*b*.1922) published his first novel, *Lucky Jim*, in 1954. Its influence, which was considerable and widespread, can be seen throughout *Billy Liar*. There are obvious differences. Jim is a young university lecturer infuriated by the pretentious, culturally snobbish behaviour and speech of the professional middle-class people around him. Billy is a clerk who has recently left school; he is infuriated by the uncultured vulgarity of the lower-middle and working-class people among whom he lives. *Lucky Jim* is a richer and more complex novel in many ways, partly because it deals with adult life. Yet there are so many points of comparison that it is obvious that Keith Waterhouse wrote with Amis's book in mind. (Many of the original reviewers commented on this; see Part 4, p. 62 below.)

Jim Dixon lives in fear that his misdeeds will be discovered and that he will lose his job. He dreams constantly of escaping to London. He lies inventively in self-defence, especially to his worst enemies, his professor's wife and son. He also derives much fun from practising deception on suitable victims. He has a soppy girlfriend from whom he has much to endure, and a far better (London) girl, elusive but fonder of him than he expects her to be. He suffers an appalling humiliation in front of an audience at the end of the novel. He is always inclined to avoid work and to waste time, and thus he makes life harder for himself. In all these ways Billy resembles him so much that situations in *Billy Liar* frequently remind us of *Lucky Jim*.

The influence of Jim's inner life on Billy's is even more telling. Jim consoles himself for the boredom and irritation of listening to his professor, for example, by daydreaming of revenge:

> He pretended to himself that he'd pick up his professor round the waist, squeeze the furry grey-blue waistcoat against him to expel the breath, run heavily with him up the steps, along the corridor to the Staff Cloakroom, and plunge the too-small feet in their capless shoes into a lavatory basin, pulling the plug once, twice, and again, stuffing the mouth with toilet paper.
>
> (Chapter 1)

Jim is not an intellectual: ideas and knowledge have little appeal to him, and he rightly abandons academic life at the end of the story; but he is very articulate, wittily inventive, conscious of language and sensitive to the absurdities of speech in people such as Professor Welch who pay no attention to their own way of speaking. Billy is the same. Jim is a mimic and actor who relieves his outrage by making faces when nobody is looking. He has a 'shot-in-the-back face', a 'Martian-invader face', a 'mandrill face', an 'Edith Sitwell face', an 'Eskimo face' and so forth. He becomes an ape, when hard-pressed. He curses Welch:

> 'You *i*gnorant clod, you *stu*pid old sod, you *ha*vering *sla*vering get . . .' Here intervened a string of unmentionables, corresponding with an oom-pah sort of effect in the orchestra. 'You *wor*dy old *tur*dy old scum, you *gri*ping old *pi*ping old bum . . .' Dixon didn't mind the obscurity of the reference, in 'piping', to Welch's recorder; he knew what he meant.
>
> (Chapter 8)

Billy cannot compete with inspired fluency on this level, but he tries, when he curses his boss in Chapter 5. Billy is less mature than Jim in letting his fantasies drift unconnected with actual life. Jim has learned to use imagery. He says of a fierce-looking crony: 'he looked more than ever like Genghis Khan meditating a purge of his captains.' But any reader who comes to *Billy Liar* immediately after *Lucky Jim* will notice scores of parallels. The two books offer a good example of how a novel can be deeply influenced by another, yet be fresh and original.

Billy Liar is one of a group of works, written in the late 1950s and the 1960s, dealing with working-class and lower-middle-class life in the provinces of England, especially in the North, and usually with young characters. John Braine (1922–86), a writer from Bradford, published his novel *Room at the Top* in 1957. Shelagh Delaney (*b*.1939), from Salford in Lancashire, wrote her play *A Taste of Honey* at the age of eighteen; it was produced in London in 1958. Alan Sillitoe (*b*.1928), from Nottingham, published his novel *Saturday Night and Sunday Morning* in 1958, and his story of a Borstal boy, *The Loneliness of the Long Distance Runner*, in 1959. John Osborne (*b*.1929), whose play *Look Back in Anger* was performed in London in 1956, can be seen as part of the immediate literary background to this group of Northern writers. With Amis, he was seen at the time as a leader of a group of 'Angry Young Men', angered by anything pompously middle-class. That term was repudiated by several of the young men (and women) so labelled; it has come to seem of little value. Further back in time and in America, James Thurber (1894–1961), whose story 'The Secret Life of Walter Mitty' was published in 1942, has been considered an influence on Waterhouse's novel – Walter Mitty is a small-town fantasist. Good novels about growing up in Yorkshire published during the 1960s include *A Kestrel for a Knave* (1968) by Barry Hines (*b*.1939), a grim story which was filmed by Ken Loach as *Kes* (1969). Details of film versions of many of these books, including *Billy Liar*, appear later in these Notes (Part 4, p. 61).

A note on the text

Billy Liar was published by Michael Joseph, London, in 1959, and by Norton, New York, in 1960. It was published in paperback by Penguin Books, Harmondsworth, Middlesex, in 1962. By 1988 this edition had been reprinted twenty-two times. *Billy Liar* the play, by Keith Waterhouse and Willis Hall, was published by Michael Joseph, London, in 1960, and by Norton, New York, in 1961. The play is summarised, and compared with the novel, in Part 4 of these Notes. Quotations from the novel are from the Penguin edition. The numbered parts of the novel are called chapters in these Notes.

Part 2

Summaries
of BILLY LIAR

A general summary

Billy Fisher lives with his parents and grandmother in the (fictional)
Yorkshire town of Stradhoughton. He left school about a year ago to
work as a clerk in a firm of undertakers. Unhappy at home and bored
at work, he wants to go to London to become a script-writer. The
comedian Danny Boon has written him a letter of mild encouragement
from London, but has not offered him a job. Neither his family nor the
people at work (except for a fellow clerk called Arthur Crabtree)
understand or sympathise with his ambitions. They are all 'ordinary
folk' (his mother's phrase), more or less content with their ordinary
lives. Billy feels different from them in many ways, but especially in the
way he uses language. Most people in Stradhoughton speak in worn
stock phrases which they consider to be natural. Billy revels in mimicry
of every kind of English he hears, but other people's clichés seem
hardly worth mocking, and he finds it hard to talk to them. Arthur
Crabtree shares something of Billy's flair and ambition. Liz, his best
girlfriend, thinks she understands him. Everyone else thinks that he is
daft.

He has been acting in a daft manner throughout the last year. Under
his bed is a Guilt Chest containing more than two hundred of the firm's
good-will calendars. They were given to him for posting nine months
ago, before Christmas last year, but Billy kept the postage money for
himself. There are also unposted invoices for his father's haulage
business and his mother's letter to Housewives' Choice. At work,
hidden in the basement, there are two nameplates for coffins, evidence
of unconfessed mistakes. His personal affairs are in disarray. He is
engaged to two of his three girlfriends: to 'sexless' Barbara ('the
Witch') and to the latest Miss Stradhoughton, the lovely but equally
gormless Rita. His third girlfriend, Liz, far superior to both her rivals,
is often away from town.

Because real life is so worrying, Billy consoles himself with fantasies
of Ambrosia, a nobler land than Yorkshire, where he is a war-hero and
Prime Minister. The habit of make-believe has spread into everyday
life, however, and he has invented family circumstances, including a
married sister and her children, to enliven otherwise boring
conversations.

Billy wakes, on the first page, determined to make decisions; the novel tells the story of his unsuccessful day. At breakfast he fails to persuade his family that he has been offered a job in London. Ridding himself of the calendars, in the lavatory at work where he partially destroys one, is as difficult as ever. In the coffee break he gives Barbara's engagement ring to Rita. The pleasure of cross-talk routines with Arthur is soured when Billy makes Arthur jealous by telling him about his 'job' with Danny Boon. Meeting the Witch at lunchtime in a graveyard in town, Billy feeds her a 'passion pill' without result and purloins a miniature silver cross from her handbag. An interview with Mr Shadrack, junior partner at the undertakers, goes badly; the firm cannot accept his letter of resignation until the missing calendars, among other matters, have been explained. Nagged at home, Billy is rude to Gran, who suffers one of her fits. Out on the moors with a heap of calendars for burial, he meets the senior partner, Councillor Duxbury, who speaks to him about his misdeeds with such kindly old-fashioned Yorkshire wisdom that Billy is for once moved to remorse and respect. He is alarmed by the Councillor's threat of speaking to his father.

Meeting the Witch at a modern cemetery in the afternoon, Billy feeds her more passion pills, confesses to some of his lies, and promises to reform. He is immediately detected in a lie by Mrs Crabtree, Arthur's mother, and escapes on a bus. Later in the afternoon he gives Barbara's silver cross to Rita. He finds Liz at the X-L Disc Bar, and they agree to meet at the Roxy dance hall in the evening; he has already invited Barbara and Rita. Performing his weekly comic turn at a pub called the New House, he sees Councillor Duxbury talking to his father. Worse follows at the Roxy: Arthur announces publicly that Billy is going to London to work for Danny Boon; Rita and Barbara (whose coffee-cup Billy fills with passion pills) have compared notes; Mr Shadrack tells Billy that he is suspended from work. Out alone with Liz, Billy tells her about Ambrosia and they make love, while spied upon by Stamp and two drunken cronies who spring up from the bushes with cries of derision. Billy leaves Liz at the Roxy where the tannoy has been calling his name all evening, and goes home to face his father. The secrets of the Guilt Chest are known. At the end of a tremendous row, Billy sets off in a taxi, his suitcase full of clothes and calendars; before reaching the railway station, he must go to the hospital where Gran is dying. He says goodbye there to his mother after Gran has died. At the station, where he buys a ticket for the night train to London, he meets first Rita, who is contemptuous, and then Liz, leaving for Doncaster. She will go with him to London if he marries her. But Billy makes terms with reality, after this evening's long series of sobering shocks. He is not old enough for marriage and he has no job to go to in London. Whistling Ambrosia's anthem, he marches home.

Detailed summaries

Chapter 1

Billy wakes to a Saturday for big decisions, but is unwilling to face facts. Lying in bed, he withdraws for a while into a daydream about Ambrosia, a land of his own invention, where he is currently a war-hero. To direct his thoughts back to the real world, he distracts himself from daydreams by counting and by reciting a biblical quotation from Psalm 23. He decides to reform his way of life, at present too lazy and muddled, starting tomorrow at the latest. Making notes on the backs of used envelopes will help, he tells himself. He has already made some notes, including a plan to write a thousand words a day of a school story; he is thirty-four thousand words behind schedule.

As he goes down to breakfast, we begin to learn about his home and family. He lives in a small suburban house, just like hundreds of thousands of others of its kind, named – although he disapproves of such an ordinary house having a name instead of just a number – Hillcrest. Next door is the garage owned by his father, Geoffrey Fisher, a haulage contractor. Billy is late for breakfast and is wearing a raincoat in place of a dressing-gown. His parents, supported by his grandmother, begin at once to criticise his behaviour. He came home too late last night. He was seen with a girl (Rita) other than his regular and approved girlfriend, Barbara (known to Billy as the Witch), who is due to come to tea tomorrow. Impenitent, Billy is bored by the criticism and irritated by the stereotyped way, repeated every morning, in which it is delivered.

He retaliates with one of his big decisions of the day, telling his parents (dishonestly, as we find out later) that he has been offered a job in London as script-writer to Danny Boon, the comedian who has recently been performing in the town, Stradhoughton, where the Fishers live. Boon has seen some of Billy's 'material' – scripts, not a term familiar to the elder Fishers – and liked it. Billy's parents disregard him, as much from incomprehension as from disbelief. Writing does not seem to them to be proper work. Left alone in the kitchen, after eating the yolk only of a cold boiled egg, Billy consoles himself with what he calls his No. 1 thinking – deliberate fantasy. Unavoidable anxieties, his No. 2 thinking, begin when he reaches his bedroom. Under his bed are two hundred and eleven calendars, concealed in his Guilt Chest. He was told to post them last Christmas, as good-will offerings to people likely to help the firm of undertakers, Shadrack and Duxbury, where he works as a clerk. He kept the postage money for himself. It is now September and he has only been able to destroy fourteen of the calendars, tearing them up and discarding them by night. Other guilty secrets in the chest include his mother's letter to Housewives' Choice, never posted, and a packet of 'passion pills', said to stimulate girls. There are also postcards from Liz, his best girl, often absent from Stradhoughton, who has the special attraction, for Billy, of being literate. Later even than usual, he leaves for work, a bunch of calendars under his pullover, wondering what he is 'going to do about everything'.

NOTES AND GLOSSARY:

Ambrosia: this land of fantasy mixes far-fetched romantic heroism (sometimes treated facetiously) with details of Billy's ordinary life. Its name is therefore appropriate. In Greek mythology *ambrosia* was the food of the gods, bestowing on them immortality (the Greek meaning of the word), so it can mean anything tasting very good. Billy would also know it as the name of a brand of tinned rice pudding

March of the Movies: an invented name for the National Anthem of Ambrosia

The Lord is my Shepherd . . .: the opening words of the twenty-third Psalm in the Bible. Billy frequently uses this quotation to drive, by its irrelevance, thoughts of Ambrosia and other fantasies out of his head. See also the Notes and glossary to Chapter 14

passe-partout: adhesive tape for mounting pictures

street-cries: Billy is thinking especially of the cries in fixed forms of words called aloud by salesmen from stalls and carts

Player's Weights: cheap cigarettes

re Captain: we learn later that Billy has told Barbara that his father was a wartime captain in the Navy

The Two Schools of Gripminster: see the Notes and glossary to Chapter 3 for the note on 'the liefulness is terrific'

Hillcrest . . . not by me: Billy uses the name, mockingly, throughout his narrative; he would not use it except sarcastically because he thinks that naming a small suburban house is vulgar

Geo.: Geoffrey

Stradhoughton Technical: a secondary school for pupils aged between

eleven and sixteen, with selective admission
based on the 'eleven plus' examination, but less
academic and more practical than a grammar
school; Billy's father, we learn in Chapter 6,
regards it as an élite school, and a bad influence
on Billy

damask: linen, with designs shown by the play of light

***When Did You Last See Your Father?*:** a very popular painting by
W. F. Yeames (1835–1918), depicting an imagi-
nary scene in the English Civil War; reproduc-
tions of it formerly hung in thousands of homes

Foley Bottoms: see Chapter 11; 'a botanic clump of nothing', this
is a place to take girls

***coup*:** a violent act to win or increase power, usually in a
political context; Billy frequently uses the term
when fearing attacks mounted on him by family,
employers and girlfriends, perhaps because of his
role as Prime Minister in Ambrosia

house rules: as though in a boarding-house

cartooner: cartoonist

rhubarb-rhubarb: in the theatrical sense of random background talk

Woodbine: a very cheap brand of cigarettes, sold in packets
of five

mucky: (*Yorkshire English*) used throughout the novel in
place of 'dirty'

once had much to say: in criticism of the vulgarity of such chairs

sarcoma: a malignant tumour

Bertrand Russell: Bertrand Arthur William, 3rd Earl Russell (1872–
1970), mathematician and philosopher, winner of
the Nobel Prize for Literature in 1950. He
became very widely known for his strong moral,
social and political views, including his champion-
ship of nuclear disarmament

Markovitch: expensive cigarettes

how dreary: her speech pleases Billy by sounding frank and
fashionable; it is, perhaps, derived from the
novels of Evelyn Waugh (see Notes and glossary
to Chapter 2)

T.B.: tuberculosis

Alderman: the title of a senior member of a city or town
council

japanned: painted shiny black

leggy: containing pictures of girls

Housewives' Choice: a radio programme of records played by request

Welwyn Garden City: a new town (1920) in Hertfordshire, north of London, one of the first 'garden cities'

Eva Peron: Eva Duarte de Perón (1919–52), wife of President Juan Domingo Perón of Argentina (1895–1974; President 1946–55, 1974). Active in social welfare, she became vastly popular

Mansion Polish: furniture polish

finger-plate: metal plate below the door-handle to prevent finger-marks on the door

Any road: (*Yorkshire English*) anyway; Billy's use of dialect is a sign of affection

---

Chapter 2

We learn more about Billy's relish for language, and distaste for its hackneyed use, as he goes to work, and we follow the flow of his thoughts. The *Stradhoughton Echo* has a column signed 'Man o' the Dales' which irritates Billy by its stale literary phrases and its false picture of a traditional Yorkshire town of stone and cobbles. (We gather that Waterhouse has invented Stradhoughton along lines typical of Yorkshire towns of the 1950s.) The Main Street, Billy relfects, is like any other in Britain, with a Woolworth's store, a 'Disc Bar', and the *Echo*'s office which looks like a public lavatory. Elsewhere there are power stations and housing estates, rather than the Romantic 'dark satanic mills' that exist in the imagination of the writer of the newspaper column. Billy composes an attack on Man o' the Dales and pictures himself as an old-fashioned Yorkshireman jabbing with the stem of his pipe to emphasise his points, sitting at the bar of an old-fashioned pub. Then he reaches the office of Shadrack and Duxbury. Young Mr Shadrack has had the traditional 'Dickensian' shop-front taken out and plate glass substituted, so that the undertakers' premises now look, Billy thinks, like a suburban chip shop. Old Councillor Duxbury has retained some of the window dressing, including a vase inscribed to a Josiah Olroyd (his name misspelled and the vase therefore rejected by his family). The sight of it reminds Billy of a mistake he had made with some coffin nameplates, another of his guilty secrets. He enters the office ninety minutes late.

His fellow clerks are (Eric) Stamp, a would-be sign writer of whom we heard briefly in Chapter 1, and Arthur (Crabtree), unlike Stamp a friend or at least an ally, but also a rival because equally determined to succeed in show business. Stamp enjoys simple jokes and talks in clichés. Arthur and Billy pass their time in rehearsing comic 'routines' which they have invented, or, perhaps, learned from radio shows. Some of these are based on life in the office, where work is not demanding. Billy tinkers with the first page, constantly rewritten, of his school story, and ponders a letter to Danny Boon. That leads him to a No. 1 daydream about London and some anxious thoughts about what it would be like there with next to no money. Councillor Duxbury's arrival provokes a routine in Yorkshire dialect, full of invented words such as 'thraiped' and old jokes about clogs. Billy gleans jokes from these sessions with Arthur, we learn, to use later in his regular Saturday night 'turn' at a local pub. Arthur sings, on Saturday nights, at the Roxy dance hall. Both write songs. Stamp tells Billy that 'Woodbine Lizzy' is back. He wonders about her: is she a free spirit, or a tart? Is he in love with her? He is proud of her shabby unconventionality.

Billy descends to the lavatory in the basement where he hopes to destroy the calendars which are still hidden under his pullover. He tears out months, one at a time, reading their moralistic quotations as he flushes them away. It is hard work, and only partly successful. Stamp rattles the door and accuses him of having a 'mucky book' with him. Mr Shadrack orders them back to their office. He arranges to see Billy after lunch, saying that it is time they had a talk – ominous words for Billy. He and Arthur go out for coffee.

NOTES AND GLOSSARY:

Man o' the Dales: typical of pseudonyms for columns on local culture in provincial newspapers. A Dalesman is a countryman in Yorkshire. Billy dislikes the old-fashioned quaintness of the name because it is affected

stocky briar: a tobacco pipe

Dark satanic mills: a quotation from *Milton* (1809–10) by William Blake (1757–1827): 'And was Jerusalem builded here,/Among these dark Satanic mills?' These are not industrial mills but mills of the mind. Blake's line is generally misunderstood by people who know only the stanza from which it comes, and not the whole poem; they take it to refer to the dark stone and harsh working conditions of mills such as those in Yorkshire during the Industrial Revolution. Billy applies the term Satanic, whimsically, to everything in Stradhoughton

fifteen bob: in the old currency (until 1972) a bob was a shilling; a tanner was sixpence; half a crown was two shillings and sixpence or 'two and six'. There were twenty shillings to a pound (or 'quid') and twelve pennies or pence to a shilling. Small coins included the sixpence, the threepenny bit, the penny and halfpenny, and (until 31 December 1960) the farthing, a quarter of a penny. The purchasing power of sterling in the Britain of 1959 is indicated by Billy's calculations later in this chapter and on the second page of Chapter 14. A pound bought more than ten times what it buys today

traditional deep breath: mocking the style of the Man o' the Dales

Dickensian: in the sense of quaintly and vaguely old architecture and design, of the sort affectionately described and pictured in illustrations in the novels – especially *The Old Curiosity Shop* (1841) – of Charles Dickens (1812–70)

Pavlov dog: Ivan Petrovitch Pavlov (1849–1936), Russian psychologist, developed his theory of a 'conditioned reflex' as a result of experiments with dogs

subs: subscriptions

weed . . .new bug: weakling . . . new boy (in the slang of early twentieth-century school stories)

Mr Bones and Mr Jones: names used in the telling of jokes in minstrel shows and other such entertainments

whole bloody *point*: Stamp does not understand that, for the purposes of Arthur and Billy, the older the jokes are the better

theatre in the round: one in which the stage is surrounded almost completely by the audience

the Embankment: by the Thames, London resort of tramps and destitute people

three and nine: three shillings and ninepence; see the note on 'fifteen bob' above

Petticoat Lane: street market in the East End of London

Councillor: the clerks think it pretentious of him to use as a title in everyday life the form of address which corresponds to his position on the town council

Lord Harewood: George Lascelles, 7th Earl of Harewood (*b*.1923), cousin to the Queen, and owner of Harewood House, a mansion near Leeds

Tha wun't: You would not; Yorkshire dialect retains the second person singular, lost in Standard English in the seventeenth century

took the Michael: took the mickey, ridiculed; *thraiped*, *bracken*, *scritten* and *gangling-iron* are invented to sound like Yorkshire dialect

clog: clogs are shoes made entirely of wood or shoes with wooden bottoms; they are the traditional sign of poverty in the North of England

ah'd nobbut: I had nothing but, I had only

change out o' fourpence: Duxbury's stories of the poverty and the low cost of living of Yorkshire forty years ago seem exaggerated

the Roxy: a dance hall; see Chapter 10

Woodchopper's Ball: 'At the Woodchoppers' Ball', a fast blues tune (1939) by Woody Herman (*b*.1913), the band-leader and clarinetist

bint: (*Arabic*) girl, young woman; English seems to have acquired this word (as slang) from its use among British troops in North Africa during the Second World War

Morecambe: a seaside town in Lancashire

bohemianism: unconventional, irregular ways of life among artists and writers

alchemist: medieval and later alchemists hoped in vain to convert baser metals into gold

Never use a preposition . . . with: the sentence breaks the rule it states; this is a schoolroom joke, but one above Stamp's head

Who's Who: a reference book, revised annually, giving bio-graphical details of distinguished persons; the second Who correctly follows the verb 'to be'

something worth having: something to steal

gingivitis: inflammation of the gums

gude . . . ill: a good heart that says no ill; Scottish pronun-ciation is imitated to give a specious air of folk wisdom

Wakefield: a Yorkshire town. Other Yorkshire towns men-tioned in the novel are Leeds, Dewsbury, Doncaster, Bradford and Harrogate

The Loved One: a novel (1948) by Evelyn Waugh (1903–66) which satirises expensive and vulgar funeral practices in California. Shadrack apparently fails to see the satire

Lady Chatterley's Lover: a novel (1928) by D. H. Lawrence (1885–1930), long banned for obscenity, reissued in New York in 1959, and in 1960 in London where it was the object of a widely publicised and unsuccessful high-court prosecution

wooden: counterfeit; usually in reference to false coin

Chapter 3

Billy and Arthur perform a satirical show as they pass through the streets. They act out the Yorkshire folk story known as 'trouble at t' mill' in which a tough old capitalist quarrels with his son who has returned to Yorkshire from university full of 'fancy talk', while their workers march up the driveway of the house intent on 'lynching t' bosses'. Billy is distracted by thoughts of his three girlfriends. Arthur warns him that his mother would like to meet the Fishers. This is a threat to Billy, who has been amusing himself by spinning lies while talking to Mrs Crabtree, inventing a sister, Sheila, married to Eric, a prosperous shopkeeper, and their two children, one with an interesting medical history. He has, moreover, told his parents that Mrs Crabtree is in hospital with a broken leg. Arthur tells him that he is a pathological liar. Billy daydreams about his socially superior London parents. The lads reach the Kit-Kat coffee-bar.

The lovely but mindless Rita, Miss Stradhoughton and the American airmen's choice for 'The Girl We Would Most Like To Crash The Sound Barrier With', presides here. She speaks entirely in jeering clichés, learned in her former job at a transport café. Billy admits to Arthur that he is now engaged to Rita as well as to Barbara. He gives Rita Barbara's engagement ring (borrowed on the pretence of having it adjusted). Pleased, Rita starts dreaming of marriage, unaware that Billy is planning the speech in which he will break their engagement. He arranges to take Rita to the Roxy dance hall this evening, although he already has a date there with Barbara. Rita, like Barbara, is also invited for tea tomorrow.

Returning to the office, Billy tells Arthur that he will soon be leaving for London to take up a job as script-writer for Danny Boon. Arthur is impressed and envious at first, then suspicious, and finally only half-believing when Billy cannot produce the letter from Boon, which he has left at home. Back at the office, Stamp interrupts Billy's thoughts of triumph in London with word of a telephone call from Barbara, the Witch. She wants to meet him in their usual place at one o'clock.

NOTES AND GLOSSARY:

Tommy Atkins: the British army's equivalent of the name Jack Tar for a sailor. Nineteenth-century recruits in the army were given a specimen form completed with the name Thomas Atkins. Rudyard Kipling (1865–1936) made the expression commonly known, in *Barrack Room Ballads* (1892): 'Oh, it's Tommy this, an' Tommy that, an' Tommy go away;/But it's "Thank you, Mister Atkins", when the band begins to play'

Max Miller: a comedian noted for his rapid delivery

allus: always

Kit-Kat café: the original Kit-Cat Club was founded in London in the earliest years of the eighteenth century by a group of noblemen and men of letters

Dick Whittington: in the legend and in pantomime he is a poor boy who goes to London to seek his fortune, accompanied by his cat – hence the point of Billy's admission to Barbara that he has not got a cat at home (Chapter 7). Dick Whittington is an obvious model for Billy. The real fourteenth-century Dick Whittington, a merchant and Lord Mayor of London, bore no resemblance to the legend. He came from Gloucestershire

The Great Northern Hotel: a large hotel of the sort built in town centres by the old railway companies

Penguins: biscuits

The liefulness is terrific: 'the ----fulness is terrific' (any word can replace 'lie') is a comic formula in the speech of Hurree Jamset Ram Singh, a schoolboy character in the boys' paper the *Magnet* and the novels of Frank Richards (pseudonym of Charles Hamilton, 1875–1961). The *Magnet* ran from 1908 to 1940. *The Two Schools at Gripminster*, Billy's projected novel, sounds exactly like a *Magnet* serial. Keith Waterhouse must have read the magazine in its last years. Frank Richards's Billy Bunter stories were still extremely popular with schoolchildren in the 1950s. The vocabulary and style of Billy's story, in Chapter 2, imitate them

summat: something

'A' picture: classification for films judged unsuitable for those under sixteen

Western Brothers: two entertainers (piano and song) noted for upper-class speech and manners

Lord Muck: a jeering reference to Arthur's imitation of the Western Brothers; Rita would use the phrase whenever she heard anything sounding socially pretentious

Tramp, tramp . . . marching: a soldiers' song of the 1914–18 war

camel-hair coat: Billy's idea of a suitable garment for a successful script-writer

Jammy bugger: lucky man
an old-fashioned look: a suspicious look

Chapter 4

The Witch's favourite rendezvous is the churchyard of dark and dismal St Botolph's; she likes the statues of little angels and the bits of soppy verse inscribed on them. Witch-like, she feels at home in graveyards and cemeteries. Billy dumps his remaining calendars out of sight. He reads over the letter of resignation which he has composed during the second session of the morning's work. He is pleased with its flattery of the partners, but nervous about his approaching interview with Mr Shadrack.

Thinking about the Witch makes him angry. She seems to be 'completely sexless', and Billy has come to dislike nearly everything about her: she is sensible, healthy, opposed to cigarettes (so that he has to pretend to smoke only five a day), and addicted to oranges. She is sentimental and sententious: he has managed to cure her of calling him 'pet lamb' (sentimentally) but not of quoting the Ten Commandments (sententiously). The bag of chocolates, brought as 'snogging fodder', is almost finished; the passion pills look more promising. When she arrives he feeds her a passion pill stuffed inside the last of his chocolates. He humours her with make-believe. Each is supposed to be absurdly jealous of the other; they question each other suspiciously as though in a children's game of courtship. Billy tells her about their dream cottage, with dream children, in Devon, far from Stradhoughton's grubby realities. She asks about her ring which, he tells her, is still at the mender's.

Among the eighteenth-century graves, he tries to kiss her, but the passion pill is slow to take effect. She thinks it is indecent to be touched and fends him off by eating oranges. Enraged, he kicks over her bag, spilling oranges and personal possessions. Penitently retrieving them, he finds and pockets a miniature silver cross, a gift from her cousin which she has promised to return 'under the jealousy pact'. Over-ruling his attempts to talk about sexual 'feelings', she exacts another meeting, to look at the shops, at four o'clock that afternoon.

NOTES AND GLOSSARY:

lych-gate:	roofed gateway into a churchyard
wayside-pulpit:	a board with a poster bearing a biblical text or 'thought for the week'
the Black Death:	this jest refers to the plague which killed over a third of the inhabitants of England in 1348–9

saw: proverb or saying

Thou shalt not . . . in vain: the third of the Ten Commandments, see the Bible, Exodus 20:7

'Fisher, pay attention . . .': the imagined words of the judge about to sentence him

Baloo: one of the titles used by officers in the junior section of the Boy Scouts, taken from *The Jungle Book* (1894) by Rudyard Kipling; Baloo is the bear who teaches the Law

poker-work: burned on wood or leather

Windsor chairs: usually dark oak, with struts in the backs

crinoline ladies: see the beginning of Chapter 1

alfo: the tall form of the eighteenth-century letter 's' is commonly confused with 'f'

mean rounded vowels: in her unsuccessful attempt to speak in a more genteel accent

His hand . . . silken knee: imagined words of the 'mucky book' in Chapter 2

Ai'm **going . . .** *or-***rainge:** mimicry of her rounded vowels. Keith Waterhouse has told us that Billy speaks in a Yorkshire accent (which he broadens for 'trouble at t'mill')

Chapter 5

Back at the office and waiting for his 'little chat' with Mr Shadrack, Billy clears out his desk. He relieves his feelings of anxiety and frustration by talking and calling aloud in a mixture of animal noises, mimicry and nonsense. He is in the middle of this foolery with Shadrack's name – 'Shaddy-shaddy-shaddy . . . Hoy! Shadders!' – when his boss comes into the room. Billy pretends to have been singing. The little chat in the inner office begins amicably with Shadrack showing his model of the coffin of the future. Next come questions about the job with Boon. Is payment in such work by the joke, or salaried? Billy cannot prevent himself from imitating the man's speech habits: 'vair, vair difficult to say'. The letter of resignation, Shadrack proceeds to say, is 'vair, vair unsatisfactory'. Various matters remain unsettled between Billy and the firm. The unposted calendars have never been accounted for. The lost goodwill is incalculable. Then there is the puzzle of the coffin nameplates. We learn – although Shadrack does not – that Billy had a nameplate remade, after an error in the original one, too late for the funeral, so that the coffin went anonymous to its grave, and both nameplates are now concealed in the basement. There are other offences. Billy has been stealing stationery and, although this has not yet been detected, pilfering stamp-money. He regards all these faults as 'misdemeanours' and speaks of being sorry for having caused 'inconvenience'. Shadrack declines, in these circumstances, to accept the resignation. He speaks of the possibility of 'legal action'. Shaken and taking small comfort from any fantasies, Billy goes home.

NOTES AND GLOSSARY:

puff, puff: he is imagining himself smoking the briar pipe appropriate for use in argument with Man o' the Dales

'Pennies from Heaven': a popular song of the later 1930s, from the Bing Crosby film *Pennies from Heaven* (1936)

Nevah . . . conflict: imitating the manner of Churchill's wartime broadcasts and quoting from the speech in which Churchill said of the fighter pilots of the R.A.F. that 'never in the field of human conflict have so many owed so much to so few'

voiceofemall: Peter Cavanagh, a radio entertainer and comic impersonator of the famous, called himself this

Joycean: the Irish novelist James Joyce (1882–1941) experimented with such distortions and adaptations of words in *Ulysses* (1922) and *Finnegans Wake* (1939)

'Abide with Me': a hymn composed by Henry Francis Lyte (1793–1847)

amateur dramatics: he means that the words were spoken in a lifeless, unconvincing manner

R.I.P.: Rest in Peace, or (*Latin*) *Requiescat in Pace* (May he – or she – rest in peace)

the unforgivable sin: the sin against the Holy Ghost cannot be forgiven, according to the Bible, Matthew 12:31–2 and Mark 3:29. There has been much discussion among biblical commentators as to what this sin is. Despair, or wilful pursuit of evil? Billy's entirely facetious remark shows knowledge of what he calls 'the theological aspects'. His knowledge and understanding are notably, perhaps surprisingly, adult in this chapter where he faces the most dangerous of his adult antagonists

Chapter 6

Late for lunch, Billy is met by the customary complaints of his mother, 'Cook, cook, cook . . .', and opposition of his father, 'Stop being so bloody cheeky'. Already unhappy and exacerbated by this treatment, he speaks with startling rudeness to his grandmother, causing his father to lose his temper, although only briefly. The parents argue about whether or not Billy should be allowed to go to London. His mother says not. While this is happening, Gran suffers one of the fits to which she has lately been subject, foaming at the mouth. Upset, Billy fights off his instinctive hope that she will die. She seems to recover. He re-reads Danny Boon's letter which offers, not a job because Boon has no staff, but only a willingness to pay for occasional gags or scripts such as are provided by 'the boys'. This seems a slender offer on the basis of which to settle in London with only nine pounds, fourteen shillings and sixpence. Billy wraps three dozen calendars in a brown paper parcel and heads for Stradhoughton Moor where he means to drop them into a pothole.

He walks to the edge of the Moor and so enters Ambrosia. Postwar reconstruction and the coming of democracy are his responsibility there. Liz, the country's first Home Secretary, is abolishing prisons. He is in the middle of a speech addressed to the President of Ambrosia when he meets Councillor Duxbury. Billy mimics the Councillor's broad dialect throughout their talk about how Stradhoughton has changed since the old days. Billy makes his speech, much rehearsed in No. 1 thinking, about 'dark satanic housing estates'. Duxbury interrupts this banter with a reference to the calendars. He speaks so mildy in rebuke of Billy's mockery of his dialect that Billy suddenly feels that here is a wise old man to whom it would be good to confess everything. Duxbury says that his partner wants Mr Fisher to be informed about what has been happening at work, and Billy hangs his head. When they part, he has a feeling of 'peace and melancholy'. He buries the calendars.

NOTES AND GLOSSARY:

melodramatics: over-excited behaviour

Josiah Olroyd lines: see the first two pages of Chapter 3

fountain pens . . . suede shoes: fancy London affectations

histrionic: theatrical

widow's mite: see the Bible, Mark 12:42, for the story of the widow who donated only two mites, a very small sum of money, but was commended because her poverty made this a generous gift. Billy's use of the phrase is sarcastic: his grandmother is very generous with her criticism of him

the Lord is my shepherd: see the Notes and glossary to Chapter 1

frame yourself: look lively!

pothole: entrance to underground caves, common in Yorkshire

Quisling: a traitor, from the name of the Norwegian Vidkun Quisling, puppet-president under the Nazi occupation in the Second World War. He was tried and shot in 1945

Dr Johnson: Samuel Johnson (1709–84), the great man of letters of his age, poet, critic, essayist, lexicographer and conversationalist

George Borrow: George Henry Borrow (1803–81), traveller and writer. Billy is thinking vaguely of 'wise old men', the phrase he uses of Councillor Duxbury a few pages later

'Appen: perhaps

bahn: going

Messiah: the oratorio by George Frederic Handel (1685–1759) is the favourite Christmas music of northern English choirs. It is an element of the folk culture of Lancashire and Yorkshire

t'bugger: a half-affectionate and half rueful term here; see Part 1, 'General background'

tufts: as though of grass, to stop one falling

capped: caught

Hopefully: in the correct sense of 'with hope', not in the vulgar sense of 'if all goes well'

sither: listen to this!

a bob: a shilling, that is twice sixpence; see Notes and glossary to Chapter 2

be thisen: by yourself

Chapter 7

In a new mood of optimism, Billy rides on the top of a bus with Barbara. She is in a bad temper, viciously unpeeling an orange. He coaxes her to take passion pills, calling them energy tablets, 'Very nice with fruit!' They ride as far as the corporation cemetery, and walk among the orderly rows of graves, the Witch delighting in the flowers, angels and verses, Billy pleased by the symmetry which implies 'a modern, healthy sort of death'. The pills have still had no effect when he tries again to start kissing. He speaks of 'repressions'.

She urges patience. Remembering the message 'see Witch re Captain' on this morning's envelope, he makes a confession: his tale of his father's having been captain of a wartime destroyer, a hero and then a prisoner of war, was all lies. He admits other minor lies for good measure: stories about the family's budgerigar Roger are false, and they have no cat. Furthermore, he has no sister. Barbara says that she has always hated lies. Billy retaliates by mentioning the silver cross which he found this morning in her handbag. She had claimed to have given it back to the cousin of whom Billy pretends to be jealous. She protests that she did give it back, and Billy is relieved to find that he is not alone in telling lies. He says that he will soon be going to London. His quip that his epitaph will read 'Here lies Billy Fisher' wins her sympathy. He promises never to tell lies again. As they leave the cemetery, hand in hand, they meet Arthur's mother. Billy introduces Barbara as his sister Sheila. Unluckily, Mrs Crabtree already knows her. He escapes on a conveniently passing bus, getting his Ambrosian repeater gun into position for firing.

NOTES AND GLOSSARY:

mock-Norman: imitating the style of architecture of the period following the Norman Conquest of England in 1066

'and implemented': suggested to him by 'cleared up and implemented', Shadrack's phrase in Chapter 5. Shadrack amused Billy there by his use without understanding of the cliché from commercial English (meaning 'put into effect')

the *Graf Spee*: in December 1939 this small German battleship attacked and damaged British merchant ships. The *Graf Spee* was then pursued by (less heavily armed) British warships until scuttled by her crew in Montevideo harbour to avoid capture

U-boats: abbreviation of (*German*) *Unterseeboot*, submarines

Chapter 8

Rita is delighted with the silver cross, although she scarcely has words in which to express delight. Billy and Arthur perform a Bible routine in her honour. Then they wander through town, offering imaginary newspapers to the evening crowds: 'War Declared!' Billy has been carrying all afternoon a gramophone record to be sold back to Maurie at the X-L Disc Bar. They visit this 'glass shambles', full of girls in tartan trousers, and youths in drainpipe trousers, the air full of competing pop and jazz. Stamp is there, teasing 'little Maurie', an earnest man who runs a youth club. Gleefully, Stamp announces that Shadrack has been investigating Billy's postage book – which will show that he has been pilfering money designated for stamps. Stamp hopes that Billy will be prosecuted and sent to a Borstal institution. He also says that Liz is upstairs. Shadrack vanishes from Billy's thoughts as he joyfully mounts the stairs to the classical music department. When he sees her in her crumpled old clothes, he catches her atmosphere, 'a sensation of singing'. She is the only girl he has ever met who knows '*how*' to grin or how to talk. They talk, and Billy feels that they know 'the whole joke about the world'. She has been away for five weeks. Where? Billy has a rule he requires himself to keep without understanding why, not to ask. He makes a date to see her at the Roxy that evening. Maurie lets him have money for his record, but speaks aggressively; he has been 'hearing' about Billy – presumably from Stamp. Billy goes off whistling because he does not care.

NOTES AND GLOSSARY:

owt: anything

Joan of Arc: the French girl of the early fifteenth century who inspired the French troops to drive out the occupying English army; burned as a witch in 1431, at about the age of nineteen, she was canonised as a saint of the Roman Catholic Church in 1920

The sexfulness is terrific: see the Notes and glossary to Chapter 3, 'the liefulness is terrific'

Lo, she is the handmaiden: this line and the following Bible routine use vaguely biblical language rather than exact quotations

contretemps: (*French*) unfortunate accident, setback

Paymer!: Paper!

buckshee: free

Under Milk Wood: a radio drama (1953) by the Welsh poet Dylan Thomas (1914–53). Set in an idyllic Welsh town, the play is 'intellectual' only by the low standards of the crowd at the X-L Disc Bar

Rag-bones!: the street cry of rag-and-bone men who, with their horses and carts, collected junk from door to door

knocked off: stolen

Borstal: a reformatory for youths below the legal age for a prison sentence

cacophonous: unpleasant-sounding
growing my thumb-nail: see the second page of Chapter 1

Chapter 9

From six o'clock until half past seven, Billy walks about town, staring in amazement at the people who live ordinary lives, content with a single identity where he needs so many. Then he goes to the New House, the pub where he does a 'turn' every Saturday night. The knowledge that Liz is in Stradhoughton intoxicates him, so that he has no need for the usual strong dose of No. 1 thinking. Passing through the public bar, he is mocked by the men who drink there. They remember his having tried to win acceptance by pretending that he had a dog for sale. They laugh at him indulgently, however, because he is 'a bugger', a term which Billy interprets to mean, this time, 'a licensed clown'. A lodge meeting of what appear to be (although not said to be) Freemasons is soon to start upstairs. Councillor Duxbury, in a chain of office, calls Billy 't' untutored apprentice' and declares that 'the craft' will keep an eye on him. Two young men from Dewsbury do a mime which it is embarrassing to watch. An old man is selling a comic paper called *Billy's Weekly Liar*. The drinkers yell and laugh when they see it. 'Billy Liar. By!'

Mounting the platform for his act, Billy is conscious of his youth; he feels excluded from the solidarity which seems to unite his adult audience. Embarking on his long slow comic monologue, delivered in a broad Yorkshire accent, he panics when he sees his father, who is no pub-goer but is here tonight because he is to join the lodge. The old man can soon be seen talking to Councillor Duxbury. Billy fluffs his act, loses his audience and leaves the stage, gunning the whole room with his Ambrosian repeater. He has disgraced himself by using a London expression. A professional singer's 'laughing song' sounds mockingly in his ears as he leaves.

NOTES AND GLOSSARY:
the Odeon and the Gaumont: cinemas
'Who'd A Thought It': a twee name, and therefore appealing to Man o' the Dales
cribbage markers: in the card game of cribbage, pegs are stuck into a board to keep the score
licensed clown: in medieval and Renaissance courts, officially appointed jesters were permitted to misbehave so long as they amused
Clavioline: a piano adapted so that the sound can be amplified

Blais . . . pray: a line from the sentimental ballad 'Bless this House' by May H. Brahe (*d.*1956)

nya Lard: now Lord

the Ancient Order of Stags: 'Stags' implies men on their own in this comic misnaming of a lodge of Freemasons

an untutored apprentice: 'Entered Apprentice' is the first degree of Masonry in Britain

hidden message: Masonry is characterised by secret passwords and signs. The Stags therefore wink incessantly, and speak in quaint and obscure phrases

tiled: formally in session (with the roof built)

The craft: the Freemasons

the *War Cry*: the newspaper of the Salvation Army, sold in British pubs

the *Empire News*: a Sunday newspaper which was noted for patriotic editorials and pride in the Empire

'In a Monastery Garden': a sentimental song by Albert William Ketelbey (1875–1959)

Ah'm coortin': (*exaggerated Yorkshire dialect*) I'm courting

give ower: give over, stop (Yorkshire dialect, equivalent to the Cockney *nark it*)

Chapter 10

Billy does not expect to find Barbara at the Roxy, after the fiasco at the cemetery in the afternoon. He hopes to avoid Rita, but finds her already inside with Stamp who must have paid for her. Arthur, with a group called the Rockets, wears an American suit and sings in an American accent the song he and Billy have composed. Liz asks Billy about his plans. Seeing Shadrack, and sensing that Barbara is also present, Billy fears that his enemies are closing in. He and Arthur quarrel after Arthur has announced publicly that Billy is soon to be working in London for Danny Boon. The Hokey-Cokey is announced. Barbara has found Rita wearing the silver cross. Each has learned that the other is invited to Billy's house for tea the next day. Billy explains that he deals in miniature crosses at work. He happened to have half a dozen to spare. He cancels the invitations to tea. Dropping a handful of passion pills into Barbara's cup of coffee, he leaves, not quite avoiding Stamp, who drunkenly gloats, '*You've had it*'. Liz tells Billy that the Man o' the Dales column is written by a young journalist who is here tonight. Billy pretends to know him. The tannoy calls his name: he is wanted on the telephone. Shadrack says that the firm has suspended him, until all the explaining has been done. Billy and Liz go for a walk.

NOTES AND GLOSSARY:

the attitude of the visiting poet: looking detached and superior

cha-cha: a lively dance of Latin American origin

Moorish: of Arab, especially North African, design

foxtrot: an American ballroom dance, imported in the 1920s and still popular in the 1950s

rigor mortis: (*Latin*) the stiffness of the body in death

Danny Kaye: stage name of Daniel Kaminsky (1913–87), American stage, radio and film actor of great versatility

the Palladium: a London theatre known for variety shows

Shepheard's hotel in Cairo: catering for English customers, it became a well-known haunt of officers during the Second World War. It was blown up during an anti-British riot in 1952

Gay Gordons . . . swords: she swings her skirt as a Scotsman would his kilt for this traditional dance or for dancing on crossed swords; he means that she is sexually unappealing

Can't get along . . .: Billy's lyric is derivative and old-fashioned, deserving Arthur's harsh comment

You made me . . . do it: quoted because a classic early twentieth-century song (lyric by Joseph McCarthy)

Glenn Miller: the great American band-leader (1904–44)

Hokey-Cokey: a dance of the 1940s, with gesticulation, ending in a mêlée

Corinthian column: fluted and highly decorated in the manner of the Corinthian order of Greek architecture

academic niceties: he means precise words

Unitarians: the Protestant sect which denies the doctrine of the Trinity. Billy is 'gabbling' here, talking nonsense

naval reunion: Harrogate is a Yorkshire spa

the cub-mistress: the Baloo mentioned in Chapter 4

het up: upset

barney: row

the Boston Two-Step: this dance continues the unremitting emphasis on the American influence on provincial entertainment in Britain in the 1950s

change out of fourpence: referring to Councillor Duxbury's nostalgia for low prices in the old days

fountain pen . . . suede shoes: the thought of Man o' the Dales, whose Yorkshire would be symbolised by a dip-and-scratch pen and clogs, reminds Billy of his

	father's hostility, in Chapter 6, to these symbols of the decadence of London and all its ways
hacking:	riding a horse over roads or fields for pleasure

Chapter 11

Night falls, lamps are lit, old men leave their benches and children the builders' sand. Two youths, friends of Stamp, banned for previous bad behaviour, are refused admission at the Roxy. Billy strolls with Liz to the edge of the town. They talk of the phrase 'turning over a new leaf'; Billy wishes it meant something in real life. He would need to turn over a volume or a whole library. Life is too complicated for simple fresh starts. Liz supplies a different image: he is a child afraid of the cold water of real life. He says that he is attracted by the anonymity of London: one is too much exposed to everyone's attention in Stradhoughton. She asks if he really knows Man o' the Dales. After prevaricating, he admits reluctantly that he does not.

They reach Foley Bottoms, a patch of shabby greenery on the way to a housing estate, where he came the night before with Rita. They talk of marriage. Liz wants to marry him without delay. Tonight? Next week, she proposes. Unwilling, this time, to commit himself, he says he gets engaged too often. He suspects that there is someone hiding in the bushes: perhaps the Witch, taking notes in shorthand, or Stamp with his camera. Hitherto, their physical relations have gone 'thus-far-and-no-further'. Liz suggests that they abandon restraint. Billy decides that Shadrack has now joined the audience in the bushes. Liz admits that she is no longer a virgin. He asks her about her trips away from town. They are ways of escape, she says. She would like to have the power to be invisible. Billy has never dreamed of that, but the idea pleases him because it seems akin to his longings, and he talks about Ambrosia. They share a daydream of living together with a common escape-route into Ambrosia. He asks her to marry him. 'Tomorrow,' she says. They make love.

The sound of breaking twigs is heard in the bushes. Billy chases Stamp and the two youths who were turned away from the Roxy. Stamp calls out in derision Billy's words from his make-believe with Liz. Returning to town, the thought of Stamp and everyone else appals Billy.

NOTES AND GLOSSARY:

gaffers:	retired working-men
Mr Bones:	see the Notes and glossary to Chapter 2
high-pitched voice:	because the 'routine' in which Billy says 'I cannot

tell a lie' is based on the story of the truthfulness
of George Washington as a boy
Gregg shorthand: an alternative to the Pitman method, devised by
J. R. Gregg and published in 1888

Chapter 12

Billy escorts Liz to the Roxy. He hears his name called on the tannoy
as he waits outside while she fetches her handbag. He decides that Liz
will not come out. No. 1 thinking and a bag of chips help him home,
despite an unpleasant moment at the fish-and-chip shop, where the
manager is a man about whom Billy has recently spread the rumour
that he has hanged himself. In the No. 1 thoughts, Billy is M.P. for
Stradhoughton, writing from Westminster on parliamentary matters
to Mr Shadrack and Councillor Duxbury.

At home his father waits, nursing his wrath. His mother has wanted
him at the hospital where Gran is very poorly. They have been
telephoning the Roxy half the night. Billy is told to call a taxi. He is
forbidden to go upstairs. What has he done with his mother's letter to
Housewives' Choice? Why is it in the chest in his room? Trying to
calculate all the implications of this discovery, Billy replies that he
posted a rewritten, improved version of the letter. His father has
been listening to all that Councillor Duxbury has to tell. He knows
about the calendars. Enraged and baffled, father and son shout at
each other. Billy shouts that his father is to blame for putting him to
work with the undertakers. His father shouts that Billy is half-witted:
'like a bloody Mary Ann'. Then their anger wears out and they bicker
as usual. Who is to run the garage when he is gone, Mr Fisher
demands, and Billy thinks once more of 'trouble at t' mill'.

In his bedroom, he finds that the Guilt Chest has been rifled. He
pictures himself in London, and counts his money: nine pounds,
seven shillings. He packs a suitcase with clothes and calendars. The
taxi is at the door.

NOTES AND GLOSSARY:
pass-outs: tickets showing payment for the evening, issued
to those leaving the dance hall but intending to
return later
nix: nothing
in the committee stage: the stage at which a bill is discussed before it
passes through parliament
Tizer: a fizzy, non-alcoholic drink
clean newspaper: for wrapping up the fish and chips
daymare: daytime nightmare

coup:	see the Notes and glossary to Chapter 1
bambis:	sentimentally represented young deer
Gothic writing:	old, heavy style of print face, formerly used for German, still used for certificates
nowt:	nothing
gormless:	idiotic
get:	wretch
Mary Ann:	simpleton
chelping:	talking rubbish
A.B.C.:	a chain of cafés

Chapter 13

In the taxi Billy pretends that the driver is a chauffeur driving his Bentley towards the country pub in the Home Counties where they will stop for lunch. He chats to the driver about Gran's being poorly. The driver thinks her a grand old lass. At the Infirmary he sees groups of local women grumbling about home and hospital conditions; they are quite without the warm confidence he envied in the women enjoying themselves at the New Place earlier in the evening. His mother sits alone. In remorseless detail, she relates what has happened in the course of the evening, cherishing each banality of this major event of her life in a manner almost insufferable to Billy, who does his best to listen. In her last delirium, Gran returned in her mind to an earlier time of her life, remembering her husband and saying, 'I love you Jack'. The word 'love' sounds strange on his mother's lips, like a new invention. Billy struggles to look 'adult and sad'. He notices that while his mother tells the story he is merely her listener; when it ends, he is Billy again, and she asks about the unposted letter to Housewives' Choice. He offers the same excuse he gave his father. Why has he invented a sister? He will have to account for a cardigan, sent as a present for this sister by Arthur's mother who has telephoned on the subject. Barbara and Mrs Crabtree will be coming round tomorrow.

This news prompts Billy to say that he is going to London. Trouble cannot be left behind, his mother says, talking like a calendar, it goes with you in your suitcase. Billy thinks guiltily of the contents of his case, of which she is, of course, unaware. A nurse summons Mrs Fisher. Billy looks at fatuous jokes in a newspaper. When his mother reappears, she and the doctor escorting her look as though they are playing parts in a television serial about a hospital. Billy prays to be able to feel something. Gran has died. Mrs Fisher consoles herself by speaking in the sort of clichés she has heard on such 'corny' television shows. Billy can 'only marvel at the clichés that she used like crutches'. Billy urges that the funeral be managed by the Co-op. He prepares to leave. 'We need you at home,' his mother pleads. As he leaves, Billy 'translates' what has happened into a narrative in the style of popular fiction from the *Reader's Digest*.

NOTES AND GLOSSARY:

litany:	a prayer recited by a priest with responses from the congregation. Billy means that each time one of the women in the group speaks the others answer in chorus
she's badly:	she's very ill
giving her cheek:	speaking rudely to her
a divi:	a dividend paid to customers of a co-operative society
editorial 'we':	she speaks of herself in the plural

Chapter 14

The end of the war has left Ambrosia weak, and the treacherous Dr Grover has undermined Billy's plan for a new city. Thoughts of real life gradually break into this daydream. How is he to survive in London on nine pounds minus the rail fare?

Saturday evening is coming to an end as buses and taxis take their last passengers home. Billy walks with his suitcase to the railway station and buys a ticket to London. It is ten to one, three quarters of an hour before the train leaves. In the waiting-room, among the soldiers and prostitutes, Rita is trying to persuade Stamp, now extremely drunk, to go home. She tells Billy that she still has the engagement ring, stressing that he gave it to her; she abuses him in foul language. Stamp warns him of retribution at the office next week.

Billy sees Liz boarding a local train. He pretends to be drunk but does not deceive her. They tell each other what has been happening. Liz found Barbara in the Ladies at the Roxy, sick from passion pills. She will only come to London if Billy marries her, she tells him, and for a moment he pictures the registry office and the rented room in Chelsea. They agree to exchange postcards, and she boards the train for Doncaster.

Billy takes two armfuls of calendars from his case and dumps them, with most of the other relics of his Stradhoughton life up to now, letters from Barbara, passion pills, fragments of scripts, in the rubbish bin in the station hall. With fourteen minutes still to go before the departure of the train for London, Billy's mind mingles Ambrosia, Stradhoughton and London and verses from the twenty-third Psalm. When the departure of the train is announced, he dithers, then leaves the station and, whistling Ambrosia's anthem, starts for home.

NOTES AND GLOSSARY:
Dad, I shall want the van: addressed to the alternative father
C.O.'s p'rade: Commanding Officer's parade
Double!:   at the double, quickly!
He restoreth . . . sake: Psalm 23:3
Yea, though I walk . . . evil: Psalm 23:4

Part 3

Commentary

Nature, purpose and achievement

Billy Liar is a very funny, entertaining short novel with a memorable hero. It has a serious theme in showing the troubles of an imaginative youngster in a grim, cultureless provincial setting. The novel is well constructed, its rapid succession of scenes making a slight but effective story. It is very well written, both in Billy's bright stream of thoughts and fancies and in the dialogue. It does not pretend to be a major novel. Social problems are not explored at length or in depth; it has not the originality of Kingsley Amis's *Lucky Jim*, to which it is indebted (See Part 1, 'Literary background'). But it is more vivid, strong and sure than many more pretentious novels, especially in Billy's remarkable *joie de vivre*, his joyful vivacity which helped the story to succeed as a play, a musical and a film.

The first point Keith Waterhouse would probably want to be made about his novel is that it is funny. Billy would not be a hero without his sense of fun and his ability to make us laugh. He loves Liz for her grin: she, alone of all the girls he has met, knows '*how* to grin, or anything about it' (Chapter 8). He has a touch of the faith of some of the greatest comic characters in literature, who deny the real world because they believe that life is or ought to be a comedy, and ought to have a happy ending, no matter what lies have been told to complicate the plot. Stradhoughton never seems likely to give Billy a happy ending. *Billy Liar* has a place among the novels of protest of the 1950s for its picture of Stradhoughton, a typical English provincial town, losing its individuality without caring or noticing, complacently accepting cheap, mass-produced goods, buildings and entertainment. The people speak in clichés because their minds are closed. They have no more initiative in their language than in their lives. One Yorkshireman at the New House recognises that Billy is an eccentric and a true entertainer, but the crowd prefer the smooth, inane 'laughing song' which mocks Billy as he leaves at the end of Chapter 9. He remarks, in a depressed moment while watching people in the street, that 'your blunt Yorkshire individuals are in fact interchangeable, like spare wheels' (Chapter 5). Waterhouse's Stradhoughton is trying to impose an inhuman conformity on its inhabitants. Billy, the nonconformist, is the novelist's champion because with all his faults he is at least a would-be rebel against that.

The elements of the comedy, all neatly worked together, are simple and traditional, and reasonably true to life. Billy has three girls, two unsatisfactory, in different ways, and the third elusive; amusement arises from his deceptions. Any adventurous youth might need to stretch the truth in such a situation; Billy is more blatant than most, and this particular day brings together scenes with all three girls at a rate unusual in real life; as always in farce, the scenes are contrived. Conflict with parents – normal to some degree in adolescence, but here taken to an extreme – complicates the farce, and so does trouble at work. Both types of conflict alternate and interact with his trouble with the girls. Our sense that Billy is in the wrong, insolent to his parents, a petty thief at work, is balanced by the ludicrous but poignant sufferings which result from his behaviour. The burden of calendars under Billy's pullover is laid down (in a pothole) only when Councillor Duxbury has passed sentence and offered his words of wisdom. Two other themes are counterpointed. Throughout the story there is a quick and easy escape from troubles into Ambrosia (although the land of fantasies, like a radio-station, is sometimes closed down at night by Billy's mental exhaustion); London is the real chance of escape, and Danny Boon's letter with its tantalising half-promise beckons Billy, as the bells called Dick Whittington. Grandma's death quietens the laughter which perhaps threatens Waterhouse's serious points about the stifling and demoralising effects of provincial life. It also reflects on Billy's jokes about coffins and graves. Shadrack and Duxbury are finally condemned when he urges his mother to choose the Co-op instead for Gran's funeral. Gran's death prepares us for the ending, which is not one of farce, since Billy loses his job, his hope of London, Liz, at least for the present, and Rita and the Witch, and the secrets of the Guilt Chest. Nothing founded on lies remains at the close; all Billy's failures coalesce. Everything in the story has led to the inevitable conclusion when in the last lines he bravely heads for home.

Keith Waterhouse has shown an artist's sense of proportions, and kept his novel under sensible control. There is a note of senti-mentality in the scene between Billy and Duxbury and another in his love scene with Liz. Both are kept in check: Duxbury is not allowed to become a wise father-figure; Stamp's cries of derision end the understanding with Liz. Gran's death is notably free from any note of sentiment, except those which are satirised in the artificial speeches of Billy's mother at the hospital. The best jokes begin to wear thin towards the end, but the book finishes before we tire of them. Some readers may feel that we do not learn how Billy's problems can be resolved. What horrors await him on Monday morning? It is here that the novelist has been shrewdest in accepting limits to what he could undertake. The relationship between Billy and his father turns serious in their last row, when the father, instead of blustering and threatening, makes an appeal to which Billy cannot respond. Their difficulties, which are partly based on language (discussed below in the section on Language and style), could not be further explored without moving too far away from the breezy light comedy of the opening chapters. The mother's inarticulateness in the hospital begins to give her a quality of pathos which is disturbing to the essentially farcical character of Billy's misadventures. Both characters risk growing too big for their roles, and end where they should. There is no solution for Billy, except that like all adolescents he has somehow to grow up. The same good judgement appears in the restraint of the author's strictures on what he plainly finds dispiriting in the social and cultural life he shows. He is more effective because he does not allow Billy to talk like an 'angry young man'.

Background to composition

Arthur annoys Billy at the Roxy by singing in an American accent the song they have composed together. The saturation of popular entertainment by American music, songs, films and entertainers is one of the incidental satirical points of the book. It is incidental because the lack of competing English voices is a more serious complaint. Arthur threatens to sing the song in a Yorkshire accent, and Liz says that he 'could do worse' (Chapter 10). But Yorkshire accents, dialect, stories, comic 'routines' all seem funny and hopelessly old-fashioned to the younger generation of characters; their epitome is Councillor Duxbury, and when Billy learns that he can be taken seriously this comes as a surprise. Liverpool was to send singers to America in a few years' time, but in the late 1950s American voices sounded modern to teenagers in the English provinces, while their own accents did not.

Billy's impression of Stradhoughton is that whatever is traditional is disappearing: trams, cobblestones, clogs, the 'Dickensian' shop window at Shadrack and Duxbury's, coffins with brass handles, if Shadrack has his way, because he will americanise his undertaking business (Waugh's *The Loved One* is on his desk as a source of good ideas), and introduce 'a contemporary coffin', streamlined (and American) in design. Billy, being so young, is inclined to laugh at anything out of date; but he finds that new developments in Stradhoughton are equally depressing and devoid of any local character. Moorgate, the centre of town, is 'exactly like any other

High Street in Great Britain' (Chapter 2). It has the same Woolworth's store, the same Odeon cinema, the same Roxy dance hall, the same X-L Disc Bar as anywhere else. On the outskirts semi-detached houses are appearing, here like everywhere else, leaving many a 'botanic clump of nothing' such as Foley Bottoms, neither rural nor urban, as a place for squalid romance. These observations and this sense of a dreary new England cause Billy to repeat his lines about dark satanic power stations and dark satanic housing estates. Blake's 'dark Satanic mills' in 'Milton' are mills of the mind, but most people imagine this very famous line (see Notes and glossary to Chapter 2 in Part 2 above) to refer to the grimy and cruel mills of the Industrial Revolution. 'Dark satanic mills I can put up with,' says Billy. The poverty and hardship of the old Yorkshire are unreal to him, something to be mocked in satirical 'trouble at t' mill' sketches. The modest degree of socialist welfare and commercial prosperity achieved in Britain in the decade after 1945 (so that Harold Macmillan could win a general election for the Conservative Party in 1959, the year of *Billy Liar*'s publication, using the slogan 'You've Never Had It So Good') has protected Billy's generation from the common pre-war sense of gratitude for any job, which can sometimes be heard in what his parents say about earning a living. Billy and Arthur seem to have no political views. Billy once (in Chapter 1) has an idea of talking seriously with Bertrand Russell, but his plans for Ambrosia are innocent of any political colouring except a vague belief in democracy. He has, indeed, no theory and no principles of any kind, but a strong feeling of dissatisfaction with the dullness of the provincial scene.

Billy, like Arthur, is typical of the lower and lower-middle classes in his generation, in having ambitions which his parents mistrust. His mother's letter to Housewives' Choice mentions that her son is a song-writer but supposes that he has 'not much chance' because 'we are just ordinary folk' (Chapter 1). This infuriates Billy so much that he never posts the letter. 'Ordinary folk' is the concept he most dislikes. He is confident that he can succeed in London, if only he can establish himself there. London, in his thoughts, is 'modern' and therefore represents a realm of opportunity even more exciting than Ambrosia.

We can try to see through Billy's story to Keith Waterhouse's own experience in the late 1940s and early 1950s, leaving school at fifteen to do odd jobs before joining the staff of a Yorkshire newspaper, then moving south to Fleet Street. But Billy is too indistinct a character for us to be able to take very seriously the claim made on the jacket of the Penguin edition of the novel that he is 'a hero for our times'. His vague ambitions and frustrations are typical of many teenagers of the period after the Second World War, which helps to explain the novel's great popular success. But Waterhouse meant us to see him as a figure representing the dreaminess and irresponsibility known to us all at some stage of adolescence. At that age, we are vague about many things, including the history of our time. So is Billy.

Structure

Billy Liar is a well-made novel. The story advances clearly from beginning to end. Everything serves a necessary purpose. Good organisation is helped by a classical simplicity of design. The ancient Greek and Latin dramatists and their French and English imitators in the seventeenth and eighteenth centuries held that a play should occupy a single limited space of time (preferably within one day), be restricted to events in one place, and have one action or story. Waterhouse observes these so-called dramatic unities. We witness one day in Billy's life in Stradhoughton. The only digressions and excursions are within Billy's mind.

The narrative point of view is a first-person recollection of the recent past. We cannot tell just how long ago this disastrous day occurred. Billy says that Danny Boon was not so well known then as he is now (Chapter 1); there are other indications that the Billy telling the story is years rather than months older than his younger self who told the lies (see the section on Characters, p. 48 below). The narrator is, however, close to the character, rather than distanced ironically by self-criticism, as Pip is, when narrating his early life in Dickens's *Great Expectations* (1860), for example. Billy remembers and sympathises with his thoughts and feelings as though it all happened yesterday.

The first chapter sets everything in motion. Billy's second engagement (the night before) to Rita, and the letter he has received from Danny Boon, have provoked a crisis which, unless solved today, will lead to disaster. He must continue to deceive his girlfriends. He must dispose of the calendars and other contents of the Guilt Chest, thus continuing to deceive his family and employers. He must resign and, if need be, escape from his job, and deceive friends, family and even himself into believing that Danny Boon has offered him a job, if he is to leave for London. To act, he must fend off, or use only to sustain his morale, thoughts of Ambrosia. By the end of the day, all these aims will be in ruins.

Saturday suits the novel's scheme because it allows scenes at work, at the office in the morning, supposedly working, and with Shadrack after lunch, attempting to resign; scenes at home, at breakfast and at the late lunchtime when Grandma has her fit; scenes with the girls, in the afternoon as well as in the mid-morning and lunchtime breaks from work; and scenes at the pub and dance-hall in the evening. Very little needs to happen. Billy resigns; Shadrack speaks to Duxbury, who speaks to Mr Fisher. Liz returns (and leaves again). Grandma has a fit and dies. Billy's lies spin out the rest of the story.

Accounts of the novel sometimes say that Billy 'lives in a world of fantasy', or imply that he spends most of his time daydreaming. It is revealing to see how little of the text is actually occupied by passages in which Billy is indulging in fantasy. In the first chapter Ambrosia fills half the first page; fifteen pages later there is approximately a page of No. 1 thinking about the alternative parents. The second chapter begins with a page and a half of fantasy about Man o' the Dales; six pages later there is half a page of fantasy followed by half a page of realistic thinking about London. Five pages later there are seven lines about Ambrosia. Three pages into the third chapter there is a 'brief morning bulletin' of No. 1 thinking, about the alternative parents. The next bulletin, even briefer, involving Man o' the Dales, is on the first page of Chapter 5 which finishes with five lines of No. 1 thinking. There is one page about Ambrosia in Chapter 6. From this point on, fantasy becomes rarer until Billy returns to Ambrosia on the first page of the last chapter. The arrival of Liz frees him, he says, from the need for excursions into No. 1. His fantasy of Man o' the Dales collapses in Chapter 10. This is of course Billy's busy day: he spends most of his time grappling with practical problems or with other people. The novel's art lies in giving prominence to the passages of fantasy, and in placing them in such a way that we have the impression of Billy as a dreamer as well as a liar. Much of the text is devoted to the staging (this is a staged novel, inviting dramatisation) of scenes – at breakfast, in the office – which are connected and briefly interrupted by 'interior monologue', that is to say, by Billy's thoughts, and by his reports to us of his past and present habits of thinking.

Language and style

Much of the variety of language and style comes from Billy's love of words. His fantasies about Ambrosia are not just a negative escape from the awkward situations he makes for himself. They are also opportunities to spin out narrative in strong sure sentences free from anyone else's interference. In the Ambrosian passage on the novel's first page, for example, there is a confidence in rhythm and diction, a happy flow of words, which contrasts with the broken phrases with which Billy forces himself back to reality in the next paragraph, and is also a contrast to the tired, frayed language in which he has to talk to his parents. As Billy's imagination sends the regiments marching through Town Square, 'no flag flew more proudly than the tattered blue star of the Ambrosian Federation, the standard we had carried into battle', the uplifting cadences echo the boys' adventure stories from which they, and the romantic but not quite serious heroism of Ambrosian campaigning, at least in part derive ('out of two thousand who went into battle, only seven remained' – of Billy's own Ambrosian Grand Yeomanry).

The school story which he fancies he is writing, *The Two Schools at Gripminster*, is another remnant of recent childhood reading: 'Sammy's second name was appropriate – for the face of this sturdy young fellow was as brown as a berry' (Chapter 2). Billy has grown out of this juvenile level of entertainment and he cannot sustain the school story beyond the first page, which he is constantly rewriting; but he enjoys distracting himself in the most tedious moments of office life with his fluency in a familiar style. Arthur likes to quote a phrase from the school stories of Frank Richards: 'The liefulness is terrific' (Chapter 3). Billy can do more than quote: he enjoys the sense of achievement which he has from reproducing the style because his work as a clerk is so dull and restricting.

Billy enjoys the peculiarities of every style he knows, and he mimics them with a youthful mixture of curiosity, satire and amusement. He half-admires the alternative parents of his No. 1 thinking, socially superior and liberal about teenage independence. He sets them talking in phrases he knows from books and radio plays rather than from life. 'Oh God, how dreary!' cries his No. 1 mother when he comes home drunk. As for leaving 'the old nest', his No. 1 father takes him to the library for a chat about 'the money end' (Chapter 1). Nearer home, the column in the local newspaper which praises traditional Stradhoughton has irritated Billy, but he remembers phrases from Man o' the Dales and mocks them as he daydreams of arguments with the Man. His best invention of this kind is 'dark satanic housing estates', with which he bores Arthur Crabtree throughout the day. Arthur sees only the obvious satirical point that industrial towns today are not like those of William Blake's eighteenth-century England. Billy likes the clash of connotations between two levels of language. Blake is poetic and intense; housing estates sound drab and prosaic; the new combination is intriguing. He succumbs to the style of Man o' the Dales, however, when he pictures their arguments in a pub, the Man 'propping his leather-patched elbows on the seasoned bar' (Chapter 2). When we learn during the evening, in Chapter 10, that the journalist who calls himself Man o' the Dales is not a weathered old countryman who believes what he writes about traditional Yorkshire, but a cub-reporter little more than Billy's age, it seems a good joke with various implications. One is that journalism has conventions of style which Billy might be learning on the staff of a newspaper, instead of wasting his days at the undertakers'. Another example of how the peculiarity of any style of writing, however banal, can fascinate him, is the appeal of the improving thoughts on the pages of the calendar which he tears up and tries to flush away in the lavatory. 'Those who bring sunshine into the lives of others cannot keep it from themselves', read and dispatched in the second chapter, is quoted by Billy in the third when Arthur is puzzled by his friend's high spirits. Cinema and radio supply other species of talk which amuse Billy. The news that Liz is 'back in town' makes him think of Westerns: 'City limits', 'Get out of town' (Chapter 2). Daydreaming of his Prime Ministership in Chapter 6, he echoes Hollywood on politics: 'Democracy is a stranger to Ambrosia', but Billy 'will not rest' until that situation is put right.

One positive good in his daydreams is the attention he pays to language; in this respect they are rehearsals for his cross-talk routines with Arthur. The liveliest of all these is 'trouble at t' mill' where the prim affected tones of an undergraduate son clash with the northern frankness of the old mill-owner while the men from the mill march up to lynch them both (Chapter 3). Councillor Duxbury's dialect feeds other routines in which Billy and Arthur use stage-Yorkshire voices: '*Coun*cillor Duxbury. Tha wun't call Lord Harewood mister, would tha?' (Chapter 2). It is hard to tell whether this is a gem, too good not to be frequently quoted, from the Councillor's lips, or an inspired parody of his small-town self-importance. The invented Yorkshire dialect words, in which Billy and Arthur claim to be 'just about thraiped', 'bracken' or 'scritten' and in need of the 'gangling-iron', are so convincing that Waterhouse has to keep reminding us that the terms are inventions. Other routines come from music-halls by way of the radio, especially, perhaps, from the brilliant Goon Show in which Peter Sellers led a team of mimics who could twist every sort of public discourse into zany nonsense. The Bible routine in Chapter 8 is typical of Goonish amusement at the silliness of bad jokes. Hysterical reiteration of very old bad jokes ('this rod will be curtains for you') was another feature of the Goons, copied by thousands of school-children of the 1950s, including Arthur and Billy.

Whether just a way of amusing himself or a training for a script-writer's career, these routines have accustomed Billy to listen to the exact words of those whose speech exasperates him – which is to say of almost everyone else in the book. He notes how the Witch has tried to 'refine' her vowels and her vocabulary. (Billy's accent, we are to imagine, is good Yorkshire, but not 'broad'.) The result is artificial and disagreeable. Her use of the word 'unclothed' (describing how she feels without the engagement ring) is 'more obscene' he decides, than she thinks 'naked' would be. Speaking her language, Billy talks euphemistically about whether it is wrong to have sexual 'feelings'. He censors, however, her soppiest expressions, such as 'pretty please' (Chapter 4). Rita is almost refreshing as a contrast to Barbara, at least for a while: 'Oo, hark at Lord Muck!' (Chapter 3); 'Get back in the knifebox, bighead' – snapped at Arthur who has made a sharp remark (Chapter 8). All her utterances are of this sort: fixed expressions, jeering in tone, derogatory of any claim to quality of mind or feeling. Billy finds 'little meaning' in anything she says, beyond 'animal sounds'; he concludes that 'the vocabulary of human kindness' is unknown to her (Chapter 3). A far more attractive version of working-class speech is that of Duxbury. It is easy to sympathise with Billy's urge to speak it back to him. The Councillor, an able man who has sensed the political and commercial advantages of being a plain old Yorkshireman, seems to have polished up the quaintness of his 'old-worldly' way of speaking. Rebuking Billy for aping him, he pretends that his is an inferior, uneducated and outdated English; but he may really mean that *he*, not a youngster such as Billy, is privileged to speak it, as though it were some special, high-ranking tongue among 'the Stags'. The younger partner, Mr Shadrack, is characterised like a minor figure in Dickens with a few choice idiosyncrasies of speech which seem to betray an inner nastiness of nature. 'Vair, vair', he says for 'very', and Billy help-lessly echoes it; 'it is thought', he threatens, instead of 'I think', and he 'picks at words', as Billy notes: 'too much time . . . far too much time' (Chapter 2). It is because he is almost hypnotised by these quirks, and is listening to how Shadrack speaks rather than to what he is saying, that Billy ill-advisedly corrects 'anarchism' into 'ana-chronism' (brass-handled coffins in the space age) in Chapter 5.

Language is the battleground on which Billy fights his parents. He complains most of their clichés: fixed stock expressions used so often that as figures of speech or ironies they have come to sound crude to anyone who pays attention to language. His mother talks in clichés all day. 'You decided to get up, then?' she states when he is late for breakfast in the first chapter. He hears an ugly stock sarcasm, in its place in a fixed daily sequence; as a question, he reflects, it cannot be answered sensibly and politely. She means only to convey mild annoyance at his lateness; this form of words seems to her to fit that purpose. It does not occur to her to think about the words; she is not aware that people can be sensitive to 'ordinary English'. When Billy talked to his family about 'Motherisms', he complains in the first chapter, nobody knew what he was talking about. Since his replies in the same stereotyped jibes (answering 'No, I'm still in bed') are, naturally, denounced as rudeness ('cheek'), he tends to retaliate in his thoughts. He notices that his mother can launch a compound rebuke of twelve-words-in-one at him so automatically that he pretends she must time it to fit his passage from one door of the house to another (as he goes upstairs after shaving in the first chapter). When she opens her attack on his lateness at lunchtime, 'You seem to think I've nothing else to do . . .' (Chapter 6), he imagines chanting it with her as though in a theatre, or a children's game. (That his behaviour irritates her as much as her speech irritates him is a point he disregards.)

The key to what infuriates father and son with each other is given early in Chapter 6 when Billy says 'Good afternoon, father' and is told not to be 'so bloody cheeky'. A few lines later Geoffrey Fisher says of Billy's rather feeble jesting that 'if this is what they learned him at technical school, I'm glad I'm bloody ignorant'. The difference between Josiah Olroyd and his son in 'trouble at t' mill' is education. The son is home from 'Oxford and Cambridge' and therefore full of 'fancy talk' which is less than worthless in 'real life' – by which the mill-owner means business in the North of England. When Mr Fisher puts a fist against Billy's face, his son protests, 'These melodramatics', and the old man responds in fury at the 'educated' word, 'Don't melodram me with your fancy talk!' Billy is distracted from their quarrel by thinking with regret what beautiful and wasted Josiah Olroyd words these are. Simply put, in terms which Rita or Stamp would understand, Billy has learned to talk 'posh' or 'fancy', and therefore while he finds his father's speech crude or ridiculous, his father finds him affected, unmanly and unworthy of Yorkshire.

The novel does not, however, make quite such a simple opposition of educated (Standard) English against uneducated dialect. That distinction is made by the British Government report, *English for Ages 5 to 11*, from the National Curriculum Council (1988), which defines Standard English as 'the language of wider, non-regional, public communication' and discusses its being taught in schools in relation to the dialects (native and otherwise) which children speak at home. Between a dialect such as that of Duxbury and a Standard English such as that of the narrative of *Billy Liar*, there are, however, many stages of acquisition; modification and interference also complicate the question of just what is spoken in the Fisher household. The older Fishers speak Standard English modified by many features of dialect ('learned' for 'taught', 'anall' for 'indeed'), laden with clichés, limited in vocabulary (excluding most literary or academic words, such as 'melodramatic' or 'Motherism'), and, in the case of Mr Fisher, punctuated with 'bloody' (which Councillor Duxbury needs no more than Billy does). Billy has had a few more years in a better ('technical') school than his parents attended. His greed for language has helped him to benefit by learning thoroughly (although not quite mastering as his letter of resignation shows) Standard English in its spoken and written forms. (Stamp, after the same schooling, has no such proficiency.) This difference in language goes alarmingly deep. For Mr Fisher complete acceptance of Standard English would be a regional and perhaps a class betrayal. Billy knows that without it he would have no prospects in London. The novel poses in light comedy questions which are still unanswered about the use of English in Britain.

Among the Fishers dialect is strongest in the language of relationships. Billy's 'Good afternoon, father' is almost insulting. The words sound alien and hostile. Gran calls out that he needs to learn manners. Tenderness in the family requires at least a note of dialect. When Billy has a quiet word with his mother at the end of the first chapter, he says 'Any road' (for 'anyway') as a sign of affection, which is understood and accepted. In his last great row with his father, in Chapter 12, he 'harshens' his voice 'to make it acceptable': 'Why, what's up wi' me grandma?' Talking to his mother at the hospital in the next chapter, he does the same:

'I know, my dad was saying,' I said, trying to sound like his son. 'He says she's badly this time.'

But this homely phrasing, belonging to his childhood, no longer comes naturally, so that all his family dealings are under a strain.

The quality of the narrative prose, which often implies a storyteller more mature than young Billy, is a pleasure and an implicit comment on the poverty of Stradhoughton English. It has already been said in these Notes (Part 1, 'Literary background') that Kingsley Amis has influenced the style and sense of humour of Billy the narrator; in the paragraph beginning 'It was a month ago . . .', ten pages into the second chapter, for example, the capping of the phrase 'a soul-deep need' by the phrase 'tarting round the streets' is definitely Amisian. The passage which begins on the third page of the fifth chapter, 'London is a big place . . .', is a set piece, strongly influenced by Amis, and rather more adult than Billy could possibly be in the way it contemplates his animal noises with reference to linguistic effects in the novels of James Joyce. In Chapter 11, there is an attractive sentence, recalling a night with Liz on the moors, where the imagery is meant to contrast Billy's sensibility with Stamp's coarseness ('Are you getting it regular?') in the words which follow:

> On that night I had actually proposed, a pretend proposal that we had used for kindling, toasting our hands on it until the early hours when, stiff with cold, we wandered home quietly, the future spent like fireworks.

It is here that the novel is kindest to Billy's deceptions, making the proposal an act of love even though only 'pretend'.

Another implicit comment on the ugly clichés of Stradhoughton begins on the first page where the opening words of Psalm 23 are quoted from memory as a way to stop the flow of Ambrosian fantasy. On the penultimate page, as Billy's mind swarms with images, of Gran's funeral with Shadrack presiding ('vair, vair unsatisfactory') and of London on half a crown a day, the first four verses are summoned up, one at a time, to arrest Billy's thoughts:

> The Lord is my shepherd; I shall not want.
> He maketh me to lie down in green pastures: he leadeth me beside the still waters.
> He restoreth my soul: he leadeth me in the paths of righteousness for his name's sake.
> Yea, though I walk through the valley of the shadow of death, I will fear no evil . . .

These words are from the Authorised Version (otherwise called the King James Bible) of 1611. Juxtaposition of such grand and beautiful passages from the past with fragmented images of contemporary life was a feature of the poetry of T. S. Eliot (1888–1965) and of the prose of James Joyce (1882–1941). Keith Waterhouse here uses the same technique of juxtaposition, making the rich and dignified biblical language contrast with the drab clichés of Stradhoughton; the famous declaration of faith in God reminds us that none of the characters in *Billy Liar* has a firm belief of any kind.

Characters

Billy

In his Introduction to *There is a Happy Land* (see above, p. 6) Keith Waterhouse says that he left the boy in that novel without a name because he wanted every reader, remembering his or her childhood, to identify with the character. He comments with apparent regret that the fact that Billy has a name obscures the extent to which Billy is a typical teenager. 'There's a strong reader-identification in my novel *Billy Liar* because I think every adolescent goes through the kind of fantasy period which that book describes; but because I gave Billy a name I think readers tend to think of him mainly as a "character" of fiction rather than as someone with whom they share a common experience.' In the Production Note for the play *Billy Liar* Waterhouse and Willis Hall say that 'the director should not regard Billy as being a freak or a buffoon; the life of fantasy which he lives exists in most people but perhaps Billy's fantasies are nearer to the surface than most'. To some extent, then, the author intended us to see Billy as an interesting and appealing character because he is normal, rather than as the extraordinary hero he is in his fantasies: 'Genius – or Madman', he decides in the first chapter would be the title of his television profile in Ambrosia. Any adolescent with a lively mind, Waterhouse might argue, likes to think of himself this way.

Mr Fisher is sure that all such thoughts are daft. Much of Billy's daft behaviour is common practice: he is always late for breakfast and for work because he does not care for the job his father chose for him. He has quirks: slicing the top of his egg with a knife annoys his family and therefore pleases him. He has irrational fears of illness: sarcoma of the jaw or 'Fisher's yawn' is likely, he thinks, to strike any morning. Some of his fads and fetishes are leftovers from childhood: if he can walk down Cherry Row without blinking, all will be well (Chapter 1). Others, such as dropping cigarette ends into Stamp's inkwell, belong to a malcontent of any age. Billy's portrayal is accurate in showing how an adolescent tends to oscillate between childish and adult states of mind. Some of Billy's fantasies and lies are like those of a younger schoolboy; there is an element of Tom Sawyer-like mischief in his fooling of Rita and 'the Witch' (a schoolboy's nickname). At other times, as in his feeling of exclusion from the comfortable adult solidarity of the people at the New House, he suffers the painful melancholy of a later stage of growing up. In all these respects he seems normal.

Many of the characters voice opinions of Billy which imply that he is, if not a freak, something of a buffoon: 'You're shit!' screams Rita at their final meeting in the railway station (Chapter 14); 'You're like a bloody Mary Ann [half-wit],' says his father, at the end of his patience with his 'gormless young get' (Chapter 12); Liz, who loves him, says 'You're a fool' (Chapter 11); 'He's a bugger!' yells a more than half admiring man at the New House, using a Yorkshire term which often – and certainly here – contains a degree of grudging respect for an eccentric in a conformist culture (Chapter 9). 'Tha's a reet one,' says Councillor Duxbury ('a right one', one to puzzle over and remember). 'Vair, vair unsatisfactory,' mumbles Mr Shadrack (Chapter 5). Arthur, more precisely, calls him 'a pathological . . . liar' (Chapter 3), meaning one whose lies are caused by a disease of the mind. All these remarks are made in response to the annoyance the lies and deceptions have caused. Billy seems too healthy for Arthur's verdict and he is plainly too good-natured for Rita's opinion to ring true. He feels pleased at the thought that her engagement gives her a temporary happiness, even while planning the phrases with which he will break it on the grounds of incompatibility (Chapter 3). 'Solipsist' is a term Arthur might have applied to Billy, had he known it. In systems of thought termed 'solipsism' only the self is real; a solipsist ignores the real or independent existence of others. A habit of fantasy encourages this tendency. When Billy's daydreams overflow into lies, his danger is that people he has invented, his No. 1 father, the company director, or the father who was a naval hero, will be as real to him as those of flesh and blood. Even when his actual father has him by the scruff of the neck, he thinks of Father Olroyd in 'trouble at t' mill' (Chapter 6). He feels 'a little pained' to see Rita with Stamp at the Roxy because she is his fiancée 'or thought she was' (Chapter 10). The difference has become blurred in the mind of Billy Liar.

It might be said that by creating a character with whom it is often easy to identify, since his weakness is a preference we all sometimes share (for a world we can fancy over the world as it really is), and by showing how his daydreams are connected with his pilfering from work, the novel reveals how a bright youngster can become a juvenile delinquent – something that baffles Councillor Duxbury: 'Ad'd ha' thowt a lad like thee would have had more sense' (Chapter 6). A defence of Billy's theft of the stamp-money might be tried on the lines of his imagination's having run away with him. It is an obvious fact that his fluency runs away with his common sense. He is unusual in his articulateness. His lies are easiest to pardon when we sense his relish for the inviting words in which to tell them. Confronted by the combined forces of Rita and Barbara at the Roxy, Billy wonders whether he can concoct 'a piece of skilful double-talk, aimed at their different intellectual levels, that would succeed in fooling them both' (Chapter 10). His cleverness at moments such as this and his imagination at others give him an appeal which is stronger when we see him in contrast to the smug, mindless elements in Stradhoughton at its most restricting. Some readers may wish to see him as the victim of his society, forced into lies by its hypocrisies. The novel never quite authorises such a reading. However attractive Billy's deceptions, they are no more than an attractive weakness.

All the characters, including Billy, are flimsy as personalities, yet vivid in their language. Within the world of the novel, we might maintain, language therefore matters most. Billy is by far the ablest speaker and dreamer, a poet by contrast with his family, with

Shadrack, with Barbara or Rita. The regiments of Ambrosia win all their battles for Billy by the power of words. Mrs Fisher's 'We can't all be Shakespeares' is a deadening remark in its apathy. Stradhoughton agrees with her and does not care. Billy cares; he would be Shakespeare if he could. Although no poet, he is on the side of poetry, and that is why, for all his faults, he is the novel's hero.

His level of culture is mysterious. In Chapter 2 he seems to have read Evelyn Waugh's *The Loved One*; in Chapter 5 to have read and understood James Joyce; in Chapter 6 to know something about Samuel Johnson and George Borrow. His style is mature enough to reflect such a background, but his mind seems culturally more juvenile, except for the mention of these names, and it is hard to see how extended reading would fit into his way of life. We must assume that Joyce, at least, was read in the period of growing up which must have taken place between the events and the time of their narration.

Mr (Geoffrey) Fisher

Billy's father, 'the old man', is depicted by his son without affection or respect. He hates all intellectual pretensions in his son: 'bloody fountain pens', 'all them bloody papers and books and rubbish' (Chapter 6). His last row with Billy hints at his resentment that his son is not fit to learn the haulage business which he runs from the garage next to the house. A proper son, he thinks, would speak in 'blunt and blunted' phrases like his, aggressive in tone because this is the only 'acceptable' way for a man to speak. He would work in the garage. Billy is 'bloody idle' (Chapter 12). Schooling has spoilt him. (Such a father would scarcely tolerate the idea of his son staying on at school beyond the age of fifteen or so.)

Mr Fisher is not a bad man of his type. He is not physically violent. He works hard. He avoids pubs. He upholds standards of decency and politeness as he understands them. Thousands of such fathers saw their sons grow 'soft' and 'daft' and leave for London to become writers, or actors or professional men. When Mr Fisher shows contempt for script-writing as an occupation, we may be reminded of how D. H. Lawrence's father – a coal miner – was horrified to learn how much his son could earn for a piece of writing.

Mrs Fisher

Her letter to Housewives' Choice is completely typical of such letters, written by women who want to be as 'ordinary' as possible. It is this word, in the phrase which she uses proudly, 'ordinary folk', which infuriates Billy who wants to be extraordinary. For his mother, being ordinary, liking the same music on the radio, using the same expressions on the same occasions as all other ordinary folk, means being safe and respectable; for her, life offers nothing better. She is quite typical of a caring but worried and vexed mother of her background. She is afraid of Billy's fancy notions. In his resentment he thinks that nothing unfamiliar can have any meaning to her, nothing strange ever impress her. If he came home Prime Minister of Ambrosia, in full dress uniform and speaking Ambrosian, she would not be impressed. Better a safe job at Shadrack and Duxbury's.

Gran (Ma Boothroyd)

Billy resents his grandmother as a permanent guest in the house, and he dislikes the crude aggressive phrases she flings out even more than he dislikes his parents' habits of speech. She is a crabbed old woman, perhaps playing that role, conscious of the life about her and totally disapproving of Billy. There is a peculiar incivility typical of old people of her kind in having abandoned the use of names: 'He wants to give him a good hiding' (Chapter 6). Waterhouse made her as antagonistic as he could. Billy stops himself from wishing her death, after her fit; he feels nothing when she dies.

Barbara, the Witch

Barbara resembles Billy in her wish to substitute fantasy for grimy Stradhoughton realities. Life in the cottage in Devon with little Barbara and little Billy, its lily pond conjured into being by Billy's invention, almost cancelled by Barbara lest the kiddies fall in, derives from the happy ending of a story in a women's magazine. She has made her vowels genteel with unhappy results for her flat Northern voice. Her habitual eating of oranges is perhaps part of her resistance to Billy's attempts to bring sex into their relationship. So is the wilful little-girlishness of her taste for pretty rhymes and statuettes in the cemeteries (hence her nickname) where she stages her trysts with Billy. Her only sensible remark is the last she makes in Chapter 7.

Rita

It is Rita in the flesh that attracts Billy, after his sessions with the sexless Barbara. Rita in the novel hardly exists except for her repertoire of stock expressions, some of them pungent and amusing on first encounter – until we grasp the extent to which they are automatic responses to situations, empty of thought and feeling. Rita is afraid of the mockery she assumes will follow any sincere or spontaneous or individual utterance. Keith Waterhouse has emphasised in all these characterisations the degrading effect of coarse and routine expressions, robbing Mrs Fisher of her dignity as a mourner, Ma Boothroyd of the role of a grandmother for which she lacks the words. In Rita he asserts that there can be no humanity without humane language ('the vocabulary of human kindness', Chapter 3); of this, poor Rita has none.

Mr Shadrack

Dickens would have liked the connotations of Shadrack as a name for an undertaker (its biblical origin is the Shadrach who with Meshach and Abednego survived the burning fiery furnace in Daniel 3:8–30). 'Shade' and 'rack' [wrack], 'hade' [Hades] and 'drac' [Dracula] are some of the words the name suggests. Billy, in his Joycean sequence in Chapter 5, enjoys stressing the disagreeable resonance of the name by chanting travesties of it (in a technique reminiscent of Lucky Jim's curses against Welch). Shadrack has 'little notebooks' and a 'propelling pencil rattling against his teeth' (Chapter 2). He had been a car salesman and has brought appreciation of clean metallic lines to his conception of 'a contemporary coffin'. The smooth, would-be ingratiating but not quite polite manner of a car-salesman is mixed with a tone of menace in his teasing of Billy. He enjoys issuing threats at the Roxy at the end of Chapter 10.

Councillor Duxbury

While Shadrack cultivates the role of 'a new man', Duxbury enjoys playing the honest old Yorkshireman. He is shrewd enough to guess how the lads in his office will laugh at his quaintness and his talk about the invigorating hardships of the simple days of his youth; he is old and self-confident enough not to care. He is still playing his role, although not unkindly, when he talks wisely to Billy on the edge of the Moor at the end of Chapter 6.

Arthur Crabtree and Stamp

Arthur is Billy's crony and rival rather than his friend. He becomes jealous when Billy tells him of the job with Danny Boon, even though he does not quite believe in it – a good touch by the novelist. His few appearances imply that he is fundamentally a conformist; although he is almost as good a satirist as Billy, his satire is that of a professional entertainer in the making, while Billy, a true nonconformist, is made to feel an outsider in their last scene together. Stamp's oafishness seems meant to compensate for the relative refinement of the other two clerks.

Liz

The Production Note for the play stresses that although Liz is given to 'flitting' she is not a 'fey' character, but has a down-to-earth quality which she tries to transmit to Billy. She is of Billy's class but has risen above its limited horizons, the Note tells us. The actress should 'radiate warmth and generosity'. The Note's comment on Liz and Billy as lovers is useful: they are not in love 'but trying to get love from each other'. All these remarks apply equally to the Liz of the novel. Some readers may find her harder to believe in than other, nastier characters, perhaps because she is so completely the girl of Billy's dreams. Waterhouse may have thought that he needed her as part of the novel's real world to save Billy from seeming too pathetic a figure. He may already have been thinking of the film. In John Schlesinger's film of 1963, Liz was played by Julie Christie (her début) as a superior girl of the 1960s, independent in mind and in style of life.

Part 4

Hints for study

The play

The most valuable guide to Keith Waterhouse's achievement in the novel is the dramatisation he made with Willis Hall, first presented in London in 1960. The play, in three acts, adapts the novel freely, but remains close enough to be interesting, especially in its treatment of Billy's role, performed in 1960 by Albert Finney, and also in certain simplifications necessary for the stage which remind us of the variety and subtlety of the novel. The following summary shows how the story has been changed.

Act I

A note on the set, living-room, hall and garden of the Fishers' house, to which the whole action is confined, tells us that the furniture is 'quite new but in dreadful taste' and includes a 'cheap and flashy cocktail cabinet and a large television set'. Because we no longer see them from his point of view, Billy's parents have become Geoffrey and Alice (Fisher) and his grandmother has become Florence (Boothroyd). Florence is alone when the curtain rises, talking to herself. She is unwilling to see one doctor because he is 'a blackie', another because she is 'a lady doctor'. Alice and then Geoffrey come in for breakfast and talk about Billy who is still in bed. Geoffrey says that 'he wants a bloody good hiding' (not a threat he ever makes in the novel). Alice calls upstairs, as in the novel, and Billy appears in a raincoat over his pyjamas. The stage direction adds that he is 'nineteen years old and slightly built'. The family quarrels on the same lines as in the novel. Billy was home late and seen with a girl other than Barbara. He gives Rita's name. Alice says she will tell Barbara at tea this afternoon. Billy tells about his job with Danny Boon. He is not going to work, because this is his Saturday off – obviously a false claim. He is risking the sack, says Geoffrey. Geoffrey and Alice leave the house, Billy and Florence talk, each in a separate dreamworld, according to the stage direction, Florence talking about the hardships and narrow horizons of Yorkshire in the old days. Arthur arrives and immediately performs with Billy the

'trouble at t' mill' routine. Billy is wanted at work, he says. Shadrack
is going through Billy's postage book, and talking about calendars.
Billy opens a cupboard and shows the two hundred and sixty
calendars. Arthur finds the letter to Housewives' Choice. Billy boasts
of his job with Danny Boon. Arthur gives him the passion pills
(obtained in the novel from Stamp who does not appear in the play).
Billy explains that Barbara is coming this morning because she has to
be told that Geoffrey is not in the Merchant Navy and because Billy
must recover the engagement ring from her in order to return it to
Rita. 'Scruffy Lizzie' is also in town, Arthur reports. Barbara arrives
and admires the cocktail cabinet. Billy boasts that he made all the
furniture, and the garage. She asks about his sister. He confesses that
father is not on a petrol tanker (in dialogue partly drawn from his two
meetings with Barbara in the novel). He has a grannie who, although
not actually blind as he had said, is ill and may have to have her leg
off. Talk about the dream cottage and 'feelings' now follows (close to
Chapter 4 in the novel); then Barbara goes upstairs to wash the
orange juice off her hands, and Billy puts all the passion pills into the
glass of port she has been sipping. Mr Duxbury telephones. Billy tells
him that there is a simple explanation for the missing money in his
accounts; then he continues the conversation after putting down the
telephone. 'Some of us, Mr Duxbury, belong in the stars.' Barbara
has returned to her glass of port when the curtain falls.

Act 2

It is just after tea-time in the afternoon of the same day. Florence is
drinking tea from a pint pot, the others from the best tea service.
Barbara has announced that she and Billy are engaged. Billy is
talking on the telephone to Rita about the ring. It is still at the
jeweller's, he says; he curses and dials another number. Barbara does
not mind a long engagement. She will 'have to wait till bloody
Domesday' if she waits 'for that sackless article', says Geoffrey. Billy
tells Arthur to hurry to Rita's house and stop her coming to the
Fishers'. Florence complains that she is being rushed to finish her tea.
Barbara and Alice go off to wash the dishes. 'She'll take some
keeping,' Geoffrey comments on Barbara; 'she had her share of that
pork pie.' Billy is too young to marry, but too old to be messing about
with different lasses. It is at least something that he has 'not got
Barbara into trouble'. Billy is reluctant to admit that he is engaged.
Florence keeps interrupting until Billy tells her to 'belt up'. Geoffrey
loses his temper ('I'll clean-shirt him'), as he does in Chapter 6 of the
novel. Billy can go to London, or, better, into the army! Florence
slumps in her chair. She is taken upstairs. Billy tells Barbara that

Florence has been all over the world. His grandfather was in the Diplomatic Corps, before he had his leg off, and in the French Foreign Legion for nine years. He tries to get the engagement ring from Barbara who will not part with it. Rita arrives.

Billy goes into the garden, and the lights come on here as they fade in the living-room, where Barbara is peeling another orange. Rita attacks him with a volley of her most aggressive clichés: 'Look what's crawled out of the cheese', 'Get back in the knife box, big-head', 'Hark at Lord Muck'. She is angry because Billy has been seen out with another girl; she wants her ring. Billy improvises. The ring has to be sent to Bradford. Under further attack, he promises to have the ring by this evening, if only she will go now. She wants him to walk her to the bus stop. He claims he has to go to the lavatory, and promises to catch her up. Billy now enters the living-room. Barbara asks about his going to London. To distract her, he talks wildly. A new drug, so far tried only on President Eisenhower and the Duke of Windsor, is being tested on his grandmother, he explains. His father has twice been summonsed for using bad language. Geoffrey is an embittered man, made jealous by Billy's promise as a script-writer. The cupboard (containing the calendars) has been locked since Billy was four years old. Forty or fifty unpublished novels are in there. Geoffrey 'crucified himself in the attempt' to produce works of genius. Barbara is not to be diverted from her question. Why London? What about their cottage in Devon? 'It's all down south,' says Billy. Alice enters and reports that Florence is resting. Barbara tells Billy that Liz, the 'dirty girl' he used to know, is back. Alice sends Billy upstairs with a tumbler for Florence.

Alice calls the doctor and begins a talk with Barbara (a scene impossible in the novel where Billy as narrator has to witness everything). They discuss Billy's unwillingness to grow up. His mother thinks that the grammar school started all the trouble. 'That Liz,' says Barbara, 'put ideas into his head.' Barbara is a sensible lass, who believes in premarital chastity. Billy reappears and they all bicker. Billy means to grow a beard. He has political commitments to go with it, he claims. He almost went on the Aldermaston march, to support nuclear disarmament, and he accuses Alice and Barbara of never thinking about South Africa. The bickering is interrupted by the entry of Rita.

Rita demands the ring. Alice is shocked and angry. Billy speaks with formal correctness. Rita calls him a 'toffee-nosed get'. Then she notices Barbara whom she calls 'Madam Fancy-knickers'. She and Barbara squabble over which of them is engaged to Billy. The language of Barbara and Alice becomes haughtily respectable, that of Rita mocking and mildly ribald. Rita is confident of her position because she has a witness – Shirley Mitchem – who saw Billy give her the ring; she could go to the Town Hall. Billy is under-age (that is, under twenty-one), says Alice. Not last night at Foley Bottoms! 'He was over-age more like,' says Rita. Barbara is shocked and indignant. The girls are about to fight when Geoffrey comes in to announce Florence's death.

Act 3

It is evening, about half past nine, the same day, and the garden is dark. Geoffrey has spread out on the carpet the contents of Billy's cupboard. He is searching for Florence's birth certificate. Billy is out. The Fishers talk about Florence's addiction to tea and her war-time hoard of tins of condensed milk, still in her room. Alice is fretting because Rita's intrusion caused such an uproar when Florence was dying. Geoffrey reassures her. He describes the old woman's death, including the words about 'my Jack' with which Mrs Fisher describes her mother's end in the novel. He speaks tenderly until he thinks of Billy and his 'bloody' suede shoes. He tells how Billy was at home, watching Noddy, a television programme for younger children, when Mr Duxbury arrived, promising that Shadrack and Duxbury would fix everything, including tea after the funeral. Billy fled when he discovered that Duxbury was in the house. Geoffrey has learned from the undertaker about the calendars, postage money, missing petty cash and brass plate stolen from a coffin. Billy 'can't keep his hands off nothing'. He cannot go to London because Shadrack and Duxbury will waive criminal prosecution only if he remains at work until he has paid back what is owed. Alice has been too soft with Billy, says Geoffrey. There will be changes in future: Billy will not be allowed to see girls and will be expected to return home by nine o'clock each night. The parents begin to quarrel, but thoughts of Florence calm them.

As Geoffrey and Alice go to the kitchen, the lights fade in the living-room and the garden is now lit. Here Billy stands, with a garden-cane as a swagger-stick, pretending to be a senior officer addressing the Desert Shock Troops at the graveside of a great lady. Although 'limbless from the waist down', he says, she invented penicillin and radium. To this regiment she has been a friend, the Lady of the Lamp. Then, mimicking an army bugler, he hums the Last Post.

Arthur and Liz enter the garden. Arthur has told Mrs Crabtree that Billy invented the story of his grandmother's death: now he will be in trouble with his mother. He tells Liz about some of Billy's childish games. He warns Billy about 'Rita's naffing brother' who is threatening to put Billy in the Infirmary. Then he leaves. Liz and Billy chat. Their conversation follows that in Chapter 11 of the novel (at Foley Bottoms). Billy speaks of his 'imaginary country', but does not use the name it has in the novel. Liz urges him to take seriously the idea of going to London. There is a midnight train to King's Cross. She has friends in Earl's Court who will let them have a room. They agree to meet at the railway station at eleven.

Billy enters the living-room and begins the quarrel with his father which occupies Chapter 12 of the novel. Alice is present; some of his conversations with her in Chapter 13 are mixed with his row with Geoffrey. He tells his parents that he is leaving for London. Geoffrey tells him that the debt at Shadrack's must be paid first. In spite of Geoffrey's protests, Billy leaves with a suitcase full of calendars. His parents find the letter from Danny Boon (which reads exactly as in the novel). Alice frets at the thought of Billy being penniless in London, but Geoffrey has had enough of his gormless son. There are plenty of clerking jobs in London, he says. He and Alice go up to bed.

Arthur and Rita enter the garden. Rita wants her ring, while Arthur wants to take her down to Foley Bottoms for some snogging. She screams abuse up at the windows, from which Alice replies that there is someone dead in the house. The Fishers all want gassing, yells Rita. She and her brother will be round first thing in the morning.

When they have gone, Billy returns. He conducts music from the radio for a while, then starts packing the calendars back in their cupboard as the curtain falls.

The novel compared with the play

The playwrights' decision to set the entire play within the Fishers' house meant sacrificing the picture of Stradhoughton which is one of the strengths of the novel. There we see the town where market stalls on cobbled streets are yielding to plate-glass and neon lights, and where we also see the undertakers' office, the coffee-bar, dance hall, X-L Disc Bar, old graveyard of St Botolph's, and modern cemetery, foundations dug for new semi-detached houses, 'shoddy grass' at Foley Bottoms, and new roads beginning to cut into the moors. By leaving out the town, the play loses one of the themes of the novel: the replacing of an older Yorkshire, poor but tough, by a new society which is more comfortable but lacks individual character. Something of this contrast remains in the play in the suburban prosperity of the Fishers' living-room where Florence talks of the old days before hire-purchase, when food was never wasted, jobs never put at risk; but the novel's treatment of the theme is more varied, detailed and persuasive.

The play shows how much the novel owes to Billy's role as story-teller and commentator. Everything in the novel comes to us through his mind and feelings, from the first page where the Ambrosian army marches through his bedroom. Billy's fantasies have a warmth of charm and wit, in contrast to the drabness of Stradhoughton, and his narrative is so fluent, observant and amusing that we feel a respect for his ambitions: he might grow up to be a Keith Waterhouse. Billy is a more hopeless figure in the play and we lose out on his obsession with language which, in the novel, influences what we think of all the various characters. The absence of Shadrack and Duxbury from the stage robs us of two rich veins in the original comedy of language, and, of course, we listen to Billy's family without his satirical commentary. The novel asserts that although people like the Fishers have escaped from material poverty, stale and shoddy language still impoverishes their lives. The play, having no such theme, allows Florence, Geoffrey, Alice and even Barbara, a respect and sympathy which the novel's Billy never permits. This may seem more humane; but it can also seem a sentimentalising of 'honest northern folk', and so a falsification which the fictional Billy would mock with merciless enjoyment. The almost complete absence of sentimentality from the novel's treatment of Gran's death comes across even more impressively after we have watched or read the play.

The stage adaptation has fewer twists and turns of farce than the novel, but it depends on them more and handles them with less finesse. Re-reading the novel, we notice how artfully the appalling consequences of Billy's lies build up towards the end, all uncertain and to be suffered after the final page. The physical threat, in the play, of Rita's brother's arrival on the following morning is feeble by comparison. In the novel, of course, Barbara has not yet come to tea. The play's strength, as all the reviewers commented, praising Albert Finney's achievement in the part, is the character of Billy, whose comic spirit survives the adaptation and animates the funniest of the play's additions. The best of these is the picture of Geoffrey Fisher as a fanatical though thwarted novelist, sitting night after night at the manuscripts of his forty or fifty unpublished novels, 'chewing at his pen' and 'taking it out' on his wife and son 'when the words wouldn't come'; finally locking up the vast *oeuvre* in the living-room cupboard for fifteen years. The dramatic climax is Billy's last tribute to his grandmother. Here the actor must create the dignity the part requires. W. A. Darlington, reviewing the first production for the *Daily Telegraph*, wrote of Finney that 'because he has played Lysander [in Shakespeare's *A Midsummer Night's Dream*] (and for that matter [Shakespeare's] Coriolanus) he can allow Billy to show us not merely the outward absurdity of his fantasies, but their inner grandeur'.

> For instance, at the moment when he imagines himself a soldier at a military funeral, standing with bowed head and rifle reversed while he imitates the sound of bugles playing the Last Post, the actor not merely conveys the emotion which Billy has stirred up in himself, but transmits its momentary sincerity to the audience. That is real acting.

Apart from whatever inner grandeur an actor can convey, Billy on the stage has an exterior appeal, standing in his grubby raincoat over pyjamas in the vulgarly 'nice' suburban set, as a rebellious anti-hero of the time.

A few small changes are worthy of comment. The stage's Billy is alienated from his parents by having been to 'the grammar school', a point which is repeated and emphasised. He, not his father, has chosen the job at the undertakers' office. He is said to be nineteen, and is to be played by an adult. This makes a difference. In the novel, where he seems to be only a year or so from leaving school, the puerile strain in his fantasies is easier to accept in a reading of Billy as 'a normal adolescent'.

The film

John Schlesinger directed the 1963 film version. After making successful documentaries for television, his first feature film was *A Kind of Loving*, based on Stan Barstow's novel, its screenplay written by Keith Waterhouse and Willis Hall. *Billy Liar*, his next film, starred Tom Courtenay, who had made his name playing the Borstal boy Colin Smith in Tony Richardson's film *The Loneliness of the Long Distance Runner* (1962), scripted by Alan Sillitoe from his short story. Tony Richardson had directed the film (1961) of Shelagh Delaney's *A Taste of Honey*, adapted from the play by Shelagh Delaney and Tony Richardson. *Billy Liar*'s success in the cinema was thus part of a small wave of British films based on fiction and drama about young people in the provinces.

The film is closer than the play is to the novel. It has additional scenes, including an appearance by Danny Boon. Leslie Halliwell gives the film three stars (a high rating) in his *Film Guide* and calls it 'a brilliant urban comedy . . . seminal in acting, theme, direction and permissiveness'. Liz was played by Julie Christie.

Reviews of the novel

London reviewers welcomed *Billy Liar* in September 1959, and American notices were equally enthusiastic a few months later. Praise was often modified by acknowledgement of the influence of Kingsley Amis, and American critics tended to be struck by the extent of American cultural influence in Stradhoughton.

The Times (3 September 1959) called Billy a 'Walter Mitty youth', found him 'very funny' and found the book more of an entertainment than a study in social problems. The anonymous critic concluded: 'Mr Waterhouse is an obvious disciple of the Amis style though sometimes sentimental too, but his book is a serious portrait of provincial youth for [all] that' – implying that Amis's influence was perhaps frivolous. John Coleman in the *Spectator* (11 September 1959) mentions Amis and John Osborne as influences, referring to the ripping of calendars in the lavatory as a 'panic Amis incident', selects for special praise the fake dialect, approves of the comedy, but regrets a more sombre, moral tone towards the end. In the *New Statesman* (12 September 1959) Maurice Richardson wrote:

> Mr Waterhouse has a remarkable gift for projecting himself under the skin of the modern adolescent. Billy's daydreams are contemporary right up to the minute. The small town and family background is richly detailed. The writing is nice and tight. A lot of it is really funny . . .

Richardson took more seriously than Coleman the novel's aim to be something more than really funny. 'Under the harsh surface of farce, there is a good deal of human sympathy.' Among other British reviewers, the *Guardian* commended Waterhouse's satire, and *The Times Literary Supplement* his 'surrealism'.

In the United States, the *Chicago Sunday Tribune* (10 June 1960) remarked on 'the prominence of American influences in the life of a small town', and 'the massive dreariness' of life in Stradhoughton, 'the utter lack of direction and . . . hope of anything better'. This reviewer's summing up is favourable: 'another crackling, lively novel in England's new tradition of writing from the inside of the working class with spirit and ruthlessness.' Richard McLaughlin in the *Springfield Republican* (3 January 1960) praised 'the flair for spontaneous comedy', judged Billy 'always credible' and 'his plight touching'. *Time* (4 January 1960) called Billy 'a Dick Whittington who misplaces his cat and never makes it to London'. The *Saturday Review* (27 February 1960) admired 'a brilliant novel, in language fresh and sweet'.

Other reviewers, although not hostile, were more hesitant. The

Yale Review (March 1960) found the novel derivative, resembling 'at every point . . . those older and more bitter heroes of John Osborne, Kingsley Amis, Alan Sillitoe . . .' This critic saw the novel as a satire weakened by the youth of the hero:

> The cultivation of fantasy, of irresponsibility, of destructiveness by maturer men has a weight of implication that Mr Waterhouse's more innocent hero can hardly suggest. Billy is amusingly outrageous, but he is not very tellingly outraged.

Conservative disapproval of 'permissiveness' in the novel appeared in the *Christian Science Monitor* (5 January 1961): 'a combination of sex, foul language, and futility that has become all too familiar in the outbursts of today's angry young men.' This writer admits, however, that Waterhouse also offers 'a point of view that makes both the humorous and sordid passages a comment on existence rather than a neutral or resigned acceptance of it'. There was a balanced, sympathetic review by the novelist John Updike in the *New York Times* (3 January 1960). Updike praised the comic first half of the novel where 'the author gives us adolescence full-bodied, in its raucous ferocity'. Plot, he complains, makes demands in the second half which press hard on the humour. Later serious passages conflict with the comic tone. Updike concludes that he 'would not want this excellent book . . . any different', but thinks that light comedy is insufficient for the author's experiences 'and his feelings about them'.

Essay topics

(1) Why does Billy tell lies?
(2) Illustrate and discuss Billy's interest in language.
(3) Illustrate and discuss Billy's fantasies.
(4) Is it true to say that Billy lives in a world of fantasy?
(5) Is Billy unusual or abnormal in the nature or the extent of his fantasies?
(6) What do we discover from the novel about the extent of Billy's education?
(7) 'Billy should still be at school.' Do you agree?
(8) 'Billy is completely without principle.' Is this true?
(9) Is the novel realistic in showing Billy's relations with his girlfriends?
(10) Is Billy young for his age, supposing that to be about sixteen, or mature for his age, or a peculiar mixture of both?
(11) Compare Billy with any one or two adolescent character(s) in other novel(s) or play(s).

(12) Why does Billy object to the way his parents and grandmother speak?

(13) Discuss Billy's relations with his family.

(14) What does Billy dislike about Stradhoughton?

(15) Discuss Billy's attitudes to Councillor Duxbury.

(16) What would an overseas reader of today learn from the novel about life in the North of England in the 1950s?

(17) Do you think the novel 'out of date'?

(18) Discuss the novel's treatment of female characters.

(19) Could you tell from the text of the novel (ignoring the cover and title-page) that the author is a man?

(20) The theme of death is treated both comically and seriously in the novel. How well are humour and thoughts about dying combined?

(21) What does the novel tell us about social class in Britain?

(22) Give examples of dialogue which you think are particularly true to life.

(23) What is 'atmosphere' in fiction? How well does the novel create atmosphere (i) at Shadrack and Duxbury's, (ii) at the New Place, (iii) at the Roxy?

(24) What is 'verbal humour'? Illustrate your answer with examples from the novel.

(25) What are the advantages of confining the story to a single day? How does the novel introduce Billy's situation, letting us know about his past lies and deceptions?

(26) What is an 'inconclusive ending' in a novel? Do you think *Billy Liar* ends inconclusively?

(27) What do you imagine will happen to Billy in the days following the end of the novel? Justify what you say by referring to the novel.

(28) What qualities in the novel can be called 'dramatic'? Give reasons.

(29) What qualities make the novel suitable for adaptation as a film?

(30) Keith Waterhouse was more than ten years older than his character when he wrote *Billy Liar*. He was a successful freelance writer living in London. What signs of this are present in the novel (keeping in mind the way it is narrated from Billy's point of view)?

Two specimen answers

(1) Why does Billy tell lies?

Plan

a) In self-defence   b) for fun   c) because he cannot decide

a) He deceives because he dislikes his job, his home, Stradhoughton. His deceptions involve him in lying in self-defence. Examples: i) the calendars, ii) the letter to Housewives' Choice, iii) the two engagements

b) Telling lies, he comes to enjoy them. He is clever and articulate. They are extensions of his fantasies. Examples: i) lies to Mrs Crabtree, ii) lies to Barbara

c) His day for decisions is a failure. He cannot decide about London. He has no adviser. Example: lying about the job with Danny Boon

A suggested essay answer

Billy tells some lies in self-defence, others because he enjoys them, and others because he cannot decide what to do.

His lies in self-defence arise from his deceptions, and these follow from his dislike (in order of intensity) of his job, his home, and the social life of Stradhoughton. At work he feels bored and degraded; his circumstances mitigate the theft of the stamp-money for which he is punished by the burden of the calendars. Challenged by Shadrack in Chapter 5, he starts to invent a story about a fire at the Post Office. Meeting Duxbury in Chapter 6, when he is carrying a parcel of calendars out to the moors to bury them there, he says they are gramophone records. With calendars under his bed and under his jersey, he has constantly to be ready with inventions such as these. His greatest crime at home, in his parents' eyes when they find out, is his behaviour over the letter to Housewives' Choice. He tells us that he does not know why he opened it or why he then failed to post it, hoarding it instead in the Guilt Chest to be discovered in Chapter 12. The answer seems to lie in his mother's last phrase in the letter, shamefully infuriating to Billy, script-writer and hero of Ambrosia: 'We are just ordinary folk' (Chapter 1). When found out, Billy claims that he posted a rewritten, improved letter, a lie which his mother believes, although she is not placated. So far as social life is concerned the only Stradhoughton girl he really likes loathes the town as much as he does and is usually away. Barbara and Rita are caricatures of two small-town types of girl: one attractive but stupid, the other dreaming in churchyards of a 'Devon' as unreal as

Ambrosia. Irritation with each involves Billy with the other. Engaged to both, he lies again in self-defence.

Billy proposed to Rita (the night before the day of the novel, he tells us in Chapter 3) 'in an eloquent mood'. This mood frequently causes him to lie for the sheer fun of it. 'In a loose moment' (Chapter 3), he once told Arthur Crabtree's mother that he has a sister called Sheila, and in other spells of boredom he has improvised for her a husband and two children, complete with touching details, of interest to Mrs Crabtree, about his imaginary little nephew's twisted foot. Eloquence has also led him to tell Barbara that his father was a wartime hero, captured by the Germans only after his part as a naval captain in the pursuit of the *Graf Spee*. He has told her, too, of the wars between the Fishers' budgerigar, Roger, and their tabby cat. Not even the cat exists. Apologising to the Witch, he tells her that his script-writer's imagination is to blame. He seems to have retained the pleasure talkative and fanciful children sometimes take in spinning lies. Lying comes easily. He enjoys an audience. His lying extends into everyday reality the everyday fantasy life with which he consoles himself for the drab commonplaces of Stradhoughton.

Given all the difficulties of his predicament, it is not surprising that he is irresolute. His day for big decisions goes badly from the novel's first words, 'Lying in bed, I abandoned the facts again . . .' The hardest of all the facts to face is the disappointment over Danny Boon's letter, made worse by its tantalising offer and by the temptation to 'call in for a chat next time you are in London'. Billy tells his parents and Arthur and Mr Shadrack that he has been offered a job. He behaves as though that were true. He resigns. He tries to clear his Guilt Chest. But he worries about the meagreness of his savings, and his No. 1 daydreams of London are mingled with realistic fears of starving on the Embankment. It is not until the train is about to leave at half past one in the morning that he decides what to do. Is he opting for Ambrosia and a life of easy lies instead of frightening reality, or is he rightly admitting that he has lied to himself all day about the job with Danny Boon? Our answer to that depends on our reading of the novel, and cannot be definite. Billy is a failure tonight, but he is young enough to have a chance still to use his imagination to escape in a real way from Stradhoughton, and no longer be ensnared by it in the weakness of lies.

---

(2) Illustrate and discuss Billy's interest in language.

Language fascinates Billy. His comment on Stamp's way of saying 'jealous' shows both his sensitivity to the language about him, and his own ability with words:

'. . . are you jealous, eh? Eh?' He pronounced the word 'jealous' as though it were something he had dug up out of the garden, still hot and writhing.

(Chapter 2)

We see his interest in language in his comments on the speech of other characters, and in his routines and the fantasies which help him to invent and perform them.

His interest in other people's speech is mostly hostile criticism. He is irked by his father's habit of beginning sentences with 'and': 'And you can start getting bloody well dressed . . .' (Chapter 1). His mother annoys him by her almost continuous flow of clichés: 'You'll-set-off-one-of-these-days-and-meet-yourself-coming-back' is a sarcasm she flings at him after breakfast in Chapter 1. He hyphenates the whole sentence to indicate how the words are said, in one breath and mechanically, and to emphasise that they are a single fixed unit. The speakers of such stereotyped expressions in the novel rob themselves of the choice of words, and instead merely slot the appropriate phrase or sentence into the context of daily life. There is also an aggressive note in the clichés, to which Billy is very sensitive when talking to his parents, and he can mimic this exactly. They will not ask who Danny Boon is, but who Danny Boon is *when he is at home* (Chapter 1). The last phrase, from which all meaning has gone, has a jeering tone, which can also be detected in almost everything said by Rita. Billy is just as attentive to the speech of those with whom he is less emotionally involved. He notices how Shadrack repeats words pointlessly, and he says of the junior partner that he picks at words as though at spots. This conveys the absence of any love of language in such a speaker as Shadrack.

Billy, on the other hand, loves language. His fantasies of Ambrosia are signs not just of his imagination but of his fluent mimicry of styles he has come across in his reading. Ambrosian prose is uplifting – 'no flag flew more proudly than the tattered blue star of the Ambrosian Federation' (Chapter 1) – and also whimsical, as in the lines about the left-handed salute in Chapter 2. Routines shared with Arthur reveal their common interest in language and style. The invented Yorkshire dialect words are brilliant: 'thraiped', 'bracken', 'scritten', and 't' gangling iron' (Chapter 2), 'neither muckling nor mickling' (Chapter 6). The satirical sketches in the sequence they call 'trouble at t' mill' ridicule corny stereotyped situations and characters, such as the tough mill-owner Olroyd, the leader of the men, and the boss's son, home 'from Oxford and Cambridge' and an 'impudent young pup', a phrase which Billy flings at Arthur whom he has tricked into playing the role of 'the young lord and master' (Chapter 3). Billy is such a connoisseur of Yorkshire phrasing that when his father shouts at him in the middle of one of their worst rows, 'Don't melodram me with your fancy talk', he is rendered helpless by the thought 'that these were beautiful Josiah Olroyd lines' (Chapter 6). Nothing divides Mr Fisher and his son so hopelessly as the father's lack of any sense of the beauty and fun which his son finds in language.

Billy is alienated from Stradhoughton, where 'everybody I knew spoke in clichés' (Chapter 3), by his sensitivity to words. Language there, the novel asserts, has degenerated into a blunt communication system. Billy is not a genius: Arthur manages the routines, which are partly drawn from music-hall banter and from radio shows (such as the Goon Show of the late 1950s), almost as well as he can. He has the pedantry of the fairly clever schoolboy he recently was (and perhaps still ought to be). The remark about his 'grammatical pleasantry', offered to his grandmother, of which he says that he did not expect 'the fully subtlety . . . to be appreciated' (Chapter 6) sounds appropriately juvenile. But Waterhouse has given his young character his own interest and pleasure in language, and it is this, even more than his imagination, which might one day make him a writer.

Part 5

Suggestions for further reading

The text

Billy Liar is published by Penguin Books, London, in association with Michael Joseph, and by Viking Penguin, New York. It was first published by Michael Joseph, 1959.

Other novels by Keith Waterhouse

There is a Happy Land, Michael Joseph, London, 1957.
Jubb, Michael Joseph, London, 1963; Putnam, New York, 1964.
The Bucket Shop, Michael Joseph, London, 1968; as *Everything Must Go*, Putnam, New York, 1969.
Office Life, Michael Joseph, London, 1968.
Billy Liar on the Moon, Michael Joseph, London, 1975; Putnam, New York, 1976.
Maggie Muggins; or, Spring in Earl's Court, Michael Joseph, London, 1981.

Selected plays

These were all written in collaboration with Willis Hall.
Billy Liar (produced London, 1960; Los Angeles and New York, 1963), Michael Joseph, London, 1960; Norton, New York, 1961.
England, Our England (produced London, 1962, music by Dudley Moore), Evans, London, 1964.
Squat Betty (produced London, 1962; New York, 1964); included in *The Sponge Room and Squat Betty*, Evans, London, 1963.
The Sponge Room (produced London, 1962; New York, 1964). See the preceding entry.
Come Laughing Home (as *They Called the Bastard Stephen*, produced Bristol, 1964; as *Come Laughing Home*, Wimbledon, 1965), Evans, London, 1965.
Say Who You Are (produced London, 1965), Evans, London, 1966; as *Help Stamp Out Marriage* (produced New York, 1966), French, New York, 1966.

Filumena, adaptation of a play by Eduardo de Filippo (produced London, 1977; New York, 1980), Heinemann, London, 1980.

Other books by Keith Waterhouse

The Passing of the Third-Floor Buck (*Punch* sketches), Michael Joseph, London, 1974.
Mondays, Thursdays (*Daily Mirror* columns), Michael Joseph, London, 1976.
Rhubarb, Rhubarb, and Other Noises (*Daily Mirror* columns), Michael Joseph, London, 1979.

Background fiction and drama

AMIS, KINGSLEY: *Lucky Jim*, Gollancz, London, 1954; Penguin Books, Harmondsworth, 1961.
BRAINE, JOHN: *Room at the Top*, Eyre and Spottiswoode, London, 1957; Penguin Books, Harmondsworth, 1969.
DELANEY, SHELAGH: *A Taste of Honey*, Eyre Methuen, London, 1974.
HINES, BARRY: *A Kestrel for a Knave*, Michael Joseph, London, 1968; as *Kes*, Penguin Books, Harmondsworth, 1969.
OSBORNE, JOHN: *Look Back in Anger*, Faber and Faber, London, 1957.
SILLITOE, ALAN: *The Loneliness of the Long Distance Runner*, W. H. Allen, London, 1959; with *Billy Liar*, Longman, Harlow, Essex, 1966.

Critical reading on modern British fiction

BERGONZI, BERNARD: *The Situation of the Novel*, Macmillan, London, 1970, 1979.
GINDIN, JAMES: *Postwar British Fiction: New Accents and Attitudes*, Cambridge University Press, Cambridge, 1962.
LODGE, DAVID: *The Novelist at the Crossroads*, Routledge, London, 1971.
MCEWAN, NEIL: *The Survival of the Novel: British Fiction in the Later Twentieth Century*, Macmillan, London, 1981.

The author of these notes

NEIL MCEWAN was at school in Lancashire and read English at Pembroke College, Oxford. He has taught at the universities of Alberta, Leeds, Yaoundé (Cameroon), Fez (Morocco) and Qatar. He is the author of *The Survival of the Novel* (Macmillan, 1981), *Africa and the Novel* (Macmillan, 1983), *Perspective in British Historical Fiction Today* (Macmillan, 1987), and *Graham Greene* in the series 'Macmillan Modern Novelists' (1988). His most recent contribution to York Notes is *Ted Hughes: Selected Poems*. He is also the author of *Preparing for Examinations in English Literature* and *Style in English Prose* (York Handbooks).